WHILE WALKING ON WATER...

I Sank.

JOE LOMUSCIO

Here's Life Publishers

Published by
HERE'S LIFE PUBLISHERS, INC.
P.O. Box 1576
San Bernardino, CA 92402

HLP Product Number 951400
© 1986, Here's Life Publishers, Inc.
All Rights Reserved.
Printed in the United States of America

Library of Congress Cataloging-in-Publication Data
Lomuscio, Joseph, 1949-
    While walking on water — I sank.

    Bibliography: p.
    1. Success.   2. Failure (Christian theology)
I. Title.
BJ1611.2.L65   1986   248.4   86-9824
ISBN 0-89840-141-0 (pbk.)

Unless otherwise indicated, Scripture quotations are from the New International Version (NIV), © 1978 by New York International Bible Society, and are used by permission. Other Scripture quotations are from the King James Version (KJV).

FOR MORE INFORMATION, WRITE:

L.I.F.E. — P.O. Box A399, Sydney South 2000, Australia
Campus Crusade for Christ of Canada — Box 300, Vancouver, B.C. V6C 2X3, Canada
Campus Crusade for Christ — 103 Friar Street, Reading RG1 1EP, Berkshire, England
Lay Institute for Evangelism — P.O. Box 8786, Auckland 3, New Zealand
Great Commission Movement of Nigeria — P.O. Box 500, Jos, Plateau State Nigeria, West Africa
Campus Crusade for Christ International — Arrowhead Springs, San Bernardino, CA 92414, U.S.A.

To Linda

who supports me in light of my failures
and loves me in spite of my successes.

CONTENTS

FOREWORD

Joe Lomuscio has done it! He has written a book on America's most popular topic — SUCCESS!

But his message is wonderfully refreshing! Joe doesn't approach this important subject in the way that most others have done. His presentation is not merely "six steps to sure success" or "17 one-minute success capsules."

He writes about such unexpected topics as weakness and failure and falling short. But please understand that he is not advocating any of those things. This is not a manual on "How to Succeed by Failing!" He doesn't give failure an $A+$ while giving success an $F-$.

No, Joe speaks about success and failure from God's perspective. He redefines success by using what he believes is God's definition. He tells us how to turn failure into success; how to win when we end the race in 35th place, how to . . .

Let me not say any more. Let Joe tell you about it. He does it so well! As you read this book you will be helped and convicted and encouraged and blessed! And, most of all, you will be encouraged to succeed — in God's way. May God bless you as you do it!

Dr. Paul A. Cedar

PREFACE
The Success Syndrome

A recent book on success listed a number of things the reader should tell himself before reading any further. Startling as it may seem, here is the list:

- It's O.K. to be greedy.
- It's O.K. to be ambitious.
- It's O.K. to look out for number one.
- It's O.K. to have a good time.
- It's O.K. to be Machiavellian (if you get away with it).
- It's O.K. to recognize that honesty is not always the best policy (provided you don't go around saying so).
- It's O.K. to be a winner.
- And it's always O.K. to be rich.[1]

Admittedly, success is idolized today.

We have allowed the pursuit of success to become cultish in practice.

The business world demands it, and develops a dog-eat-dog arena that hardly notices the casualties. Opportunism is often the accepted rule; success is the goal, no matter what the cost, no matter who pays.

The fetish for success is a modern-day calamity that has caused us, too often, to major on minors while sacrificing quality for quantity.

A. W. Tozer's observation is even more pertinent today than when he penned it over two decades ago. He wrote, "This mania to succeed is a good thing perverted. The desire to fulfill the purpose for which we were created is of course a gift from God, but sin has twisted this impulse about and turned it into a selfish lust for first place and top honors. By this lust the whole world of mankind is driven as by a demon, and there is no escape."[2]

ONE

THAT SINKING FEELING

THE LATE AFTERNOON Little League game is still fresh in my mind. I remember being called upon to pinch hit in the last inning with our team behind. My older brother had come with a friend to watch me play. I was embarrassed when I didn't start.

Now, however, was my big chance. My brother was watching and my teammates were rooting. I grabbed my bat, spit nervously, and stepped into the batter's box. The first pitch was a called strike. I was amazed at how slow and easy-to-see the pitch was, and yet I had let it go by, almost afraid to swing.

The second pitch was virtually identical, and I winced as I heard the umpire yell "Stee-rike two!" The bat seemed to be frozen on my shoulder.

The opposing pitcher glared down at me. I glared back. His third pitch, again, was slow and over the inside part of the plate. My heart sank as the umpire bellowed "Strike three!" I slumped and turned to him in disbelief, attempting to make it look as if I was a victim of cruel circumstance, yet knowing that he had made the call correctly.

In real-life Charlie Brown style, I walked dejectedly back to the bench, dragging behind me the bat that before had seemed permanently affixed to my shoulder.

Indoubtedly, the world deals in greater problems, and I grew up to face some of them, but on that day as a Little Leaguer, I was crushed by the weight of that one failure. I was embarrassed. I had let my teammates down. I had done it in front of my brother. It was awful. It would have been a little better if I had at least struck out swinging — but I never lifted that bat from my shoulder.

That story, so vivid in my memory, seems a fitting introduction to a topic so relevant to our day. Every one of us knows what it is like to strike out. Worse yet, we all experience those days when we fail even to lift the bat off the shoulder.

What do you do when you strike out?

What is your course of action when you fall flat on your face?

How do you get a grip when everything seems to be unraveling?

It's no fun to sink, so how do you stay on top of things?

That feeling of sinking — you know how it feels, don't you? The heartache of failing. That sense of despair. The crush of losing. The agony of defeat.

Perhaps you did not get the promotion you felt you deserved.

Your daughter did not make the school band.

Your son gave up nine runs in the first inning of his first Little League start — and then was relieved by the new girl on the team.

The vacation you planned for your family was

a flop.

Whenever you try your hand at something, it backfires.

You wake up with anxiety, and you retire having received greater insight into Murphy's Law.

You want so much to stay on top of things — to walk on the water, as it were — but the waves get high, and the winds blow. Soon, like Peter, you are shouting, "Lord, save me!"

It seems that we need to be better prepared for failure, because it is a rather common experience. As someone once quipped, "If at first you don't succeed — try to hide your astonishment."

We need to understand what God's Word says about success and failure. While everyone is being coached on how to succeed, the casualty lists of those who have failed are mounting. Another manual on success is hardly needed, but rather one on failure!

Perhaps this book can be just that: challenge that will not lessen goals, or make failure desirable, but will help bring our goals into realistic perspective. My intentions are to make failure bearable and most of all — meaningful.

We all need this perspective. We need to have the pressure backed off a little. Christian sociologist Dr. Anthony Campolo, Jr., in his book, *The Success Fantasy*, writes, "Success is a shining city . . . the place of happiness. And the anxieties we suffer at the thought of not arriving there give us ulcers, heart attacks, and nervous disorders."[1]

Tozer wrote, "Excessive preoccupation with the struggle to win narrows the mind, hardens the heart, and shuts out a thousand bright visions which might be enjoyed if there were only leisure to notice them."[2]

We must be ready to benefit from failure, rather than burn out from success.

We need to be reminded that Jesus never said seek ye first place! Rather He said, "Seek ye first

the kingdom of God and His righteousness"
(Matthew 6:33).

Is it possible that because you do not have a
celebrity's testimony, cannot superintend a Sunday
school, or sing three special numbers on Sunday
evening, God deems you an outright failure? These
are the questions that need to be addressed. This
book is not (I hope) another success manual, but,
in fact, just the opposite. It is a sort of manual for
failures!

Hence, the chronic underachiever will find these
pages welcome. Our study is for those of us whose
mail always comes addressed simply "Occupant." It
is for all the spiritual Rodney Dangerfields, who
never get any respect. It is for all of us who have
not ascended to the status of a household name
(not even in our own households!) It is for all, who
in George Gobel's words, feel like brown shoes in
a world full of tuxedos.

It is for all the John Marks who, at times, utterly
fail under the demanding gaze of a successful Paul.

It is for the pastor of the church of 25 to 30
folks, who will never make the leading church growth
publications or be heard on 100 radio stations nation-
wide.

It is for the Christian who attends but rarely
attempts; who dreams but never dares; who trains
but never tries — and usually because of a fear of
failing, fear which is nurtured by the success syndrome.

A knowledge of God and His Word will help
us put everything into its proper perspective. We
will begin to sense that what the world deems success, God calls into question, while He works with
and through what the world rejects as failure. A
person filled with God's Spirit, moving in the realm
of sacrificial love and spiritual gifts, can hardly be
a failure in the record books of Heaven.

In reality, this perspective, brought about by a zeal for God rather than a lusting for success, is the only thing that will deliver us from being victims in the vortex of the success syndrome whirlpool.

The choice is ours: a life of nervous tension and fear, or one of confident abiding in the promises of God. We can be ruled by either greed or grace, by strife or the Spirit. We can have ulcers or unction. It's either "first place or else," or His kingdom first above all else. The price to be paid may be incalculable. In achieving one, we may wind up missing the other — completely.

Jess Moody set the two ideals before us in searching honesty. In his book *A Drink at Joel's Place,* he wrote:

> My church has been mentioned in several books. I have been asked to speak on national convention platforms, ministers' conferences, even executive motivational meetings.
>
> At forty-one years of age I have everything a person could want — an almost adequate salary, a beautiful parsonage, a magnificent church, a loving wife and two very normal children.
>
> The whole thing is Great Big.
>
> But lately . . .
>
> . . . in the middle of the night . . .
>
> . . . I've begun to miss something.
>
> When I was a very young minister I felt something I wish I could feel again.
>
> I heard something I wish I could hear again.
>
> It was the sound of Sandaled Feet walking beside me.
>
> Now I have convention buttons; doctors' degrees; plaques; photographs of me with movie stars, a president, and other dignitaries; fund-raising awards and dozens of other gewgaws and gadgets.

But I find myself wanting more than anything
else . . .
. . . to hear again those Quiet Steps . . .
of the Sandaled Feet.[3]

Not having the Lord to walk alongside in fellowship is too high a price to pay for fleeting worldly
success.

So we will discuss, not the type of success that
robs us of spiritual life, but the failures that can be
the greatest tools God can use to bring us into a
fullness of life.

The Holy Spirit is called the Comforter. He is
ready to come alongside and minister to us during
those especially difficult times of falling and failing.
He is the Divine Encourager. When the world jeers
at us, He will cheer for us. When we sink, He will
cause us to stand. When we are crushed, His ministry
is to console, and then cause us in turn to console
others who trip along the same path (2 Corinthians
1:3,4).

In a society that ridicules failure because of its
insatiable appetite for success, we, as Christians,
must be ready to identify compassionately with those
who fail. We must emulate our Saviour, and to those
who are sinking extend an outstretched hand.

Suggestions and Summary

- Remember that what the world calls success, often God deems a failure; and what the world scorns as failure is often acknowledged by God as success (1 Samuel 16:7; Isaiah 55:8).
- Gauge your Christian growth, not by the level of successes and failings, but on whether God's greater glory is your ultimate desire (1 Corinthians 10:31).
- Seek to be more understanding of the needs and failings of others. Consider your own shortcomings (Galatians 6:1).
- Be compassionate. Instead of pointing a finger, lend a hand (Ephesians 4:2; Galatians 6:2).
- Before moving into the next chapter, compile a list of some of the most disappointing setbacks in your life. Then next to each one jot down as many things as you can think of that you learned by experiencing that particular failure. What concepts can you now share with someone else in a similar situation?

TWO

WALKED ON THE WATER LATELY?

DO YOU EVER FEEL like Charlie Brown? His effectiveness in life was summed up once by Lucy in her typical fashion, when she said, "You, Charlie Brown, are a foul ball in the line drive of life! You're in the shadow of your own goal posts! You are a miscue! You are three putts on the eighteenth green! You are a seven-ten split in the tenth frame; a love set! You have dropped a rod and reel in the lake of life! You are a missed free throw, a shanked nine iron and a called third strike! Do you understand? Have I made myself clear?"

The Lucys of the world have indeed made themselves abundantly clear. Our imperfections and shortcomings are often well cataloged, and it is obvious that Charlie Brown is not alone.

"Your limitations are an invitation to union with all other men," wrote Michel Quoist.[1] It seems to me that he was saying something like, "Well, you failed, so welcome to the club!" Robert A. Raines put it a different way, and summed it up when he entitled his book, *Success Is a Moving Target*. Undoubtedly the poet also had this in mind when he wrote:

> Success, the mark no mortal wit
> or surest hand, can always hit.

Failure is not an abnormality in life. In fact, while success must be acknowledged as a rather exclusive club, failure is an all-inclusive one. The club includes Abraham, Noah, Moses, David, Jonah, and Peter. The roll swells with the addition of the likes of Handel, Goldsmith, Churchill, Edison, Lincoln, plus a thousand more. All of these prove one thing, as one catchy slogan has it: Success is never certain — failure is never final.

It has been stated that failures and successes are simply events that happen during the processes of a life. People who fail may in fact go on to succeed. People who succeed have usually failed and may fail even again.

Unfortunately, the credo that "nothing succeeds like success" is hyped in our society like no other. That our lives must be one continuing pattern of success is continually drilled into us by a society gone haywire, and the damage is becoming evident everywhere. There is little room for on-the-job training, and less for on-the-job mistakes.

It can be seen in the frustrated football dropout, who is now your son's Pop Warner coach, demanding athletic excellence from a ten-year-old.

Or perhaps it is your overbearing in-laws, who are certain that you will never amount to anything. They are therefore convinced that you will be depriving their unfortunate little son or daughter of all the good things in life.

It hardly makes a difference whether it is in

the business arena or on the athletic fields, displayed in best-selling books or on television commercials — the message is loud and clear: Win at all costs; no one likes a loser!

The devastating result is that many, including our teen- agers, move from one frustrating experience to another. There is so much expected, even demanded.

Women are forced into accepting a false sense of values dictated by fashion and outward appearance only. There is not much chance in a society that has grown up with Barbie dolls for someone who may look more like Raggedy Ann. Or what is in store for the young man who would love to look like a Greek god, but more closely resembles a Greek restaurant? Inferiority and low self-esteem begin to take their toll, and the walking wounded silently cry for relief.

Your junior-higher brings that kind of peer-pressure home with her. Your high-schooler becomes withdrawn, and his circle of friends grows smaller. And as parents, there's not much time to help them because your own workaday world solicits all your devotion. Competition at school, at play, or on the job has brought us near to calamity conditions. Somehow we have acquired the idea that second place is degrading and demeaning.

Henry Martin, in his syndicated cartoon strip "Good News — Bad News," humorously illustrates the pressure in the high corporate world. The scene is a room full of executives being addressed by the chairman of the board. From the podium he scowls, "As you know, Ed Watson is the idiot who let the Com-Pom account slip through our fingers. Ed, will you stand up and blither for us?" Ed's poor face is one of misery in a room full of frowns.

The sad thing is that the cartoon is too true to be funny. The Ed Watsons of our society are continually being singled out and made the object of scorn. You are expected today to have experience without experiment. You are to know without ever having had much of a chance to do.

Failure, Anthony Campolo says, is our unforgivable sin. Similarly, well-known critic of the American sports scene John R. Tunis says that losing is the great American sin.

If you have boys or girls from eight to fifteen years old, you are probably well aware that sports, next to business, has an unbridled appetite for success.

From the world of sports come phrases such as "Defeat is worse than death because you have to live with defeat." "Winning isn't everything; it's the only thing." "Nice guys finish last." And, "Show me a good loser, and I'll show you a loser."

In their book, *Winning Is Everything and Other American Myths,* Thomas Tutko and William Bruns show that this "win at all costs" philosophy is having a noticeable, damaging effect on our society.

Young players on a high school football team that lost a championship game were all given a scroll with these words by Vince Lombardi:

> "There is no room for second place. I have finished second twice in my time at Green Bay and I don't ever want to finish second again. There is a second place bowl game but it's a game *for* losers, *by* losers. It is, and always has been, an American zeal to be first in anything we do, and to win and to win."[2]

A sports writer in the Los Angeles area once commented that this type of idiocy, taken literally, has become a festering abscess racing like a runaway cancer from the Major Leagues down through the smallest Little Leagues.

It's what causes a coach, as a cartoonist depicted,

to yell at his college football team at half-time, "You guys are playing like a bunch of amateurs!"

It's this fetish for victory that has caused us as a nation to demand success in whatever we do — our businesses, our sporting events, even our wars.

Dr. Tutko writes, "We have devised an international scoreboard to chart our successes in the Olympics as well as in our wars; an obsession that was tragically reflected in our approach to Vietnam, where both President Johnson and President Nixon vowed that they were not going down in history as the 'first American President who lost a war.' "[3]

Consider the subsequent scorn heaped upon the Vietnam veterans . . . the first generation of Americans ever to lose a war! How dare they break with tradition!

That's the tragedy of the success syndrome.

It demands we win and never lose.

It demands we laugh and never cry.

It demands we run and never tire.

It demands we leap buildings in a single bound, that we run faster than a speeding bullet, that we be more powerful than a locomotive!

In a sense, it demands we walk on water! It ridicules any who would sink.

But is this really fair? Success is not a level attained. It is an experience, just like failure. Not everyone will experience it just the same way. From this perspective, success just demands too much!

Have *you* walked on water lately?

Even Peter, who literally accomplished the feat was himself a failure on numerous occasions. Besides, when was the last time anyone else walked on water?

Not an easy task to be sure. And don't you think our Lord knows that? Although He surely blesses the faith that will motivate someone to get out of the boat, nevertheless, He also knows our

frame, and remembers that we are dust. It's not that
we expect too much of ourselves, for usually we
expect too little. Rather, it is that we judge our
successes or failures by the world's standards.

I am not suggesting that we lessen our goals
or lower our sights. God forbid! I am suggesting,
though, that we set them on a realistic target — a
target that is motivated by a desire for spiritual
growth and not a passion for worldly success mea-
sured by false values. It should be one that seeks
to put into expression a clear testimony of God's
grace. One that is motivated by the ministry of the
Holy Spirit as you yield the direction of your life to
Him.

Walking on the water, as it were, may be your
goal. Fine, but if and when you begin to sink,
remember that's prime time for God to teach you as
He stretches out His hand to lift you.

A classic example of this is in the life of Elijah.
The story is found in 1 Kings 18 and 19. Elijah, on
this occasion, is the Peter of the Old Testament. He
has been walking on the water. The highest wave
lifted him to Mount Carmel, and there he was king
of the mountain. News of his triumph over the false
prophets of Baal is quick to reach Ahab and Jezebel,
and they are just as quick with threats of his destruction.

Like the sun rapidly sinking in the west, we
see Elijah dropping beneath the juniper tree, from
whence he cries out the equivalent of "Lord, save
me!" It is at this point that the angel of the Lord
says to a very tired and discouraged prophet, "The
journey is too much for you" (1 Kings 19:7). What
wonderful, honest words. You see, God knows that
it is a rough road we have to tread. He knows our
weaknesses, our limits, our needs.

It is at this point that we should consider what
might reverently be referred to as divine audacity.

It is God's daring to take risks with human weakness. His willingness to entrust to us certain jobs completely beyond our abilities.

Is it not astounding that He knows our limits, and therefore pushes us to the limit (1 Corinthians 10:13)?

He understands us and yet challenges us with knowledge too wonderful for us to comprehend (Psalm 139:6).

He wants for us ultimate success, and yet allows us to fail — and in fact gives us the freedom to fail. Even though we blow it, He can bless it. When we stumble, He straightens us up. When we sink, He can save!

I rather doubt that God expects us to move from one successful high to another. It would be nice to skip from one Mount Carmel to another, but the Lord knows that a trip down to the valley is usually very educational. God likes to speak to us in times of prosperity, but it seems He has a greater audience during times of adversity. And so it is that He would rather have us learn the best way:

through trials and tribulations,

through afflictions and disappointments,

in furnaces and on stormy seas.

We want our success without hassle. God may want success for us through heartache.

Sinking is never pleasurable, but it solicits from me a desperate cry for help — a help that only my Savior can deliver. Going down has the benefit of being raised back up, and that, in biblical terms, is what growing in relationship with the Father is all about. I think perhaps that Peter never felt closer to his Lord than when they walked back to that little ship, hand in hand — together!

Suggestions and Summary

- Failure is not necessarily losing, and success is not necessarily winning (Luke 12:16-21; Luke 18:9-14).
- We will ultimately come to realize that we will be a success only when we can live without success (Acts 20:24).
- Failure always provides the opportunity of a closeness with God. Look for Him then (Psalm 46:1; Job 22:21; Matthew 14:30,31).

THREE

THE FOLLY OF INSTANT SUCCESS

WE LIVE IN A DAY of overnight wonders. We have everything from instant coffee to instant success. Quick and easy convenience markets are on every street, and fast-food stands on every corner. We have gone from miracles to microwave ovens.

Ours is a world of drive-in markets, drive-in theaters, drive-up banks, drive-through funeral parlors, and yes, even drive-in churches.

We enjoy everything from overnight deliveries to one-day developing. We buy one-step floor wax and minute rice. Everything is:

quick,

easy,

fast

and time saving.

But whatever happened to the old-fashioned belief that the best things take time? As Christians, we are bombarded with such a steady diet of quick, commercialized successes that the instant-success syndrome is bound to carry over into our spiritual reasoning and discernment.

Success in our society is the drive to achieve based on the ability to perform. Hence, we have become discouraged when the young person we just led to the Lord cannot perform up to what we believe are accepted standards. I mean, why can't he recite all the books of the Bible; know all there is to know about the book of Revelation; and pray out loud like I can? What is taking him so long anyway? Is Stan Mooneyham correct in his diagnosis? He says that "Christians are embarrassed when others' failures contradict the image of piety and saintliness we have projected for ourselves and them. Our embarrassment produces a judgmental attitude."[1]

So we judge what we think is the problem.

We identify the failure and prescribe the solution.

And yet, the problem is not necessarily with those who are failing, as much as it is with our judging.

We expect instant disciples! And the hard, cold (and to some, even shocking) facts are that the disciples are *made,* not born! To quote Henry Foster, "The Christian does not leap forth, Minerva-like, full grown at the first instant."[2]

Why, then, must we demand instant success?

God does not. He took time — some sixteen hundred years in the writing of His great Book.

He had Moses prepare for forty years before He sent him to stand before Pharaoh.

He waited some four hundred years between Testaments, and then He sent forth His only begotten Son.

Our Lord Jesus waited another thirty years before His public ministry began in the baptismal waters of the river Jordan.

Jesus took time!

He invested long hours in the molding of a handful of men. A.B. Bruce wrote, "The careful, painstaking education of the disciples secured that the Teacher's influence on the world should be permanent; that His Kingdom should be founded on the rock of deep and indestructible convictions in the minds of the few, not on the shifting sands of superficial evanescent impressions on the minds of the many."[3]

These men were no instant disciples. Not a microwave saint in the bunch!

Peter had to go through the school of hard knocks, and so did the rest of them. It seems, however, that we would just as soon attend another school. We want things a little easier, and a whole lot quicker. Jacob's ladder may have been fine for the tough, old forefathers, but we would rather have an escalator, thank you.

We are hopeful that there must be some superspiritual, miracle potion that once it is stirred into the pot — presto! like magic — out comes a full-fledged, fully-matured and full- grown, successful saint.

We desire that so much for ourselves that we really spend great amounts of time (as well as money) in searching for just the right ingredient.

We desire that so much for our churches that we pour in all types of flashy schemes to produce growth — growth which we are sure will take place overnight, if not sooner.

But hold on! The church is not an overnight success! God desires to build an oak tree, not a mushroom. He is not desirous of some flash-in-the-pan ministry that is here today and gone tomorrow. He is not all that impressed with our get-rich-quick schemes.

Instant success is not even true of Christianity in general. Christianity has stood the test of time. It forged out a tough, hard-fought existence in its infancy in Jerusalem. It became bloodied but unbowed during the Dark Ages. It survived plagues, and death, and the onslaught of the evil one. It conquered!

Christianity is not some fleeting footstep on shifting sand. It is no flickering spark flashing itself out in an instant amid a darkened sky. It is not a firecracker — it is dynamite! (Romans 1:16).

It has been burned, hammered out, cooled off, and worked over on the anvil of the centuries.

If it is a "success" (and God has promised that ultimately it will be), it is surely not an "instant" success.

Nor shall our lives be.

The best things take time.

We must give them time.

Success, *real* success, must take time. The successful know that. They allow for it. It can be illustrated in a thousand different ways on a hundred different levels. One need only think of the Edisons who experimented time and time again; or the Michelangelos who toiled under incredible circumstances for hours on end to produce the masterpieces of this world.

A friend of Thackeray once called on him in the early evening to find him working on a single sentence. When the friend returned some four hours later, he found the great author still at work on that one sentence!

The French novelist Balzac is said to have spent a week on a single page. Bryant's "Thanatopsis" was written and rewritten a hundred times before it was presented to the world. The famous Dutch painter Gerhard Dow would spend days just painting a hand. He once devoted a whole day to painting dewdrops on a leaf of cabbage! Thomas Gray's famous "Elegy Written in a Country Churchyard" was polished for some twenty years before it was released for publication.

In light of just these few examples, Longfellow's lines take on a new challenge:

> The heights by great men reached and kept
> Were not attained by sudden flight.
> But they, while their companions slept
> Were toiling upward in the night.[4]

We are, unfortunately, so out of touch with these examples of yesterday that they seem almost other-worldly. Ours is a hurry-up world, and we dare not slow the pace.

We have settled for cop-out clauses like "that's good enough," when we know enough wasn't our best. Our rush has caused us to sacrifice the best for the merely good.

This has been passed on to our children. They not only need our advice and guidance, but they need our attention and time as well. Time, tragically, is one thing we're often too busy to give.

The infernal rush of this day has affected all areas of our lives, from reading to romance, from educating to eating, from working to playing. The world is in a great big hurry to get nowhere.

A century ago John Ruskin warned that no changing of our pace at a hundred miles an hour, nor making of things a thousand yards a minute, would be able to make us one bit stronger, happier or wiser. It was Ruskin's belief that the glory of a man is not in the going, but in the being.

A thorough study of Paul's life will reveal this characteristic that seems to be wholly missing in Christians today. He took the time to develop. Years were spent in steady growth. Paul was persistent. Paul was no firecracker — he was a dynamo! He consistently and steadily generated power. His was no flash-in-the-pan performance. It was a continual glow that endures to this day. Hence, he could exhort: "My dear brothers, stand firm. Let nothing move you. Always give yourselves fully to the work of the Lord"(1 Corinthians 15:58).

One of the most refreshing and honest admissions to be found anywhere comes from his pen in his epistle to the Philippian Christians: "I want to know Christ" (Philippians 3:10).

What makes those simple words so incredible is that they come some twenty-five years after Paul first met the Lord Jesus Christ on the road to Damascus! He sensed that in the full-orbed scheme of things he still had a lot of learning to do. He had not arrived, he had not yet attained; he, years later, was still moving steadily onward and upward.

Christianity has no instant success stories. Rather, the pattern is that men and women become "successful" through years of toil and tribulation, hard work and dedication.

The legacy of Christianity is that men and women, as they get closer to their Lord, realize greater their imperfections and failings, and desire greater heights. After knowing Him for years, they understand their need to know Him even better. They do not stop at some "success" level attained, but go past that point and usually make the most of past experiences of failure as they advance.

Suggestions and Summary

- God is not so much concerned with your ability as with your availability (Isaiah 6:8; 1 Corinthians 1:27).
- Allow time to make the important things of your life their best (Psalm 37:7,34; Galatians 1:15-18).
- Never sacrifice the best for what's merely good, no quality for quantity (Numbers 18:29-32).
- Saying "that's good enough" after a hurriedly completed project is an admission not of accomplishment but of abridgment (Malachi 1:6-14).
- To do less is to fail by that much.[5]
- Over the next week, catalog the amount of time you spend in the following areas: watching television, sleeping, eating, reading your Bible, praying, worshiping, recreation, reading the newspaper (magazines). Consider how much time is being given to the development of your spiritual life.

FOUR

GREAT MEN AND OTHER FAILURES

AN INTRIGUING PERSPECTIVE often stated is that success is nothing but failure wearing a fresh coat of paint. There is valuable and practical insight in that thought. Others have related it slightly differently, such as, "Failure is but the backdoor to success."

These are refreshing perspectives. They do not convey a distorted and flashy view of success. Rather, they put some working clothes on the process.

I believe our God has a great time in showing us that our disappointments may in fact be His appointments. God wants to show us that every exit can also be an entrance.

Upon being discharged from the Air Force, I began what I believed to be my life's work in the field of air conditioning/refrigeration mechanics. A job was waiting for me, and being in Phoenix, Arizona, the prospects of plenty of work abounded.

That first summer, however, turned to misery. I was not happy. Although I felt I was never really given a chance, my performance seemed to be less than what my boss expected, and so I was let go.

I felt bad, and in seeking the Lord, I came to realize that God never had any intention of allowing me to continue in that line of work. He had called me into the ministry, and this disappointment of mine was in reality His appointment. My exit from one job was only an entrance into a greater work.

Success is usually achieved through setbacks. We can be encouraged to know that wars can still be won even though some battles are lost. Therefore, we must come to appreciate:

victory through defeat,
attainment through abasement,
success through failure.

Such a startling possibility is this that God, in His Word, drives home the message time and time again. Such a real-life human paradox is this that history affords proof in just about any area one wishes to investigate. The fact is that some of our greatest success stories were first some of our greatest failures.

It is in just this area that the Bible is perhaps the most refreshing, as well as revealing. Even the Bible's critics admit to the uniqueness of the objective way in which it describes the personalities within its pages.

The Bible never "Hollywoods" its heroes. Bible characters are portrayed in all their humanity:

their ups and their downs,
their highs and their lows,
their failures as well as their successes.

In the pages of Scripture, we see the great King David in all his splendor — and then the squalor of his adultery and murder. We see Elijah, on fire for God atop Mount Carmel — then burned out and angry with God underneath a juniper tree.

Not only do we see Moses obedient, but also disobedient. We meet Noah, alone, righteous, and standing firm — only to see him get drunk and pass out after the flood. Samson, who fought mightily against hundreds of Philistine soldiers, fell before a single Philistine seductress.

These were all great men — men of success, if you please. Yet they were all, at some point, great failures, too!

Consider Moses.

Moses is the original if-at-first-you-don't-succeed-try-try-again story. He stands as one of the great figures in the history of mankind. A study of Moses' life, though, reveals a life fraught with failures and setbacks.

The first forty years of his life were spent mostly in obscurity. We're told that as a result of killing an Egyptian in anger, he lost his status as a member of the royal household and was forced to flee into the land of Midian, where he would stay for another forty years.

It was at the conclusion of this second forty-year period that Moses was called by God from the burning bush in the shadow of Mount Sinai.

He was reluctant — seemingly unwilling.

"Who am I, that I should go to Pharaoh?" (Exodus 3:2).

"Suppose I go to the Israelites . . . and they ask me, 'What is his name?' Then what shall I tell them?" (3:13).

"What if they do not believe me or listen to me?" (4:1).

"O LORD, I have never been eloquent. I am slow of speech and tongue" (4:10).

Of course the Lord reminds this fugitive, soon-to-be prophet, that God made his mouth. The bottom

line was that it was still God's will to use this humble
and meek man.

What follows in the career of Moses is understood only as one can understand the divine movings
of a sovereign God. Moses bursts upon the scene
with all the confidence and zeal of a seminary
graduate.

"This is what the LORD, the God of Israel, says:
'Let my people go' " (5:1).

So far, so good. But Pharaoh is not the least
bit impressed and he deflates Moses' enthusiasm
with an arrogant, "Who is the LORD, that I should
obey Him?"(v.2).

Well, after one inning the score is Pharaoh one,
Moses zero. Now let's be honest, although perhaps
our business is not as crucial as the deliverance of
Israel, we have days like that. They start off bad
and progressively get worse. There is no letup to
the disappointments, and the score piles up against
us. We are shot down at work, or fed up at home.
The pressure mounts and giving up seems the sen-
sible thing to do. Quitting in the face of those types
of difficulties and failings, though, produces dead-
ness and robs us of the potential miracles to come.

As for Moses, the drama unfolds. Things do
not seem to get much better, no matter how many
times he tries to persuade Pharaoh. After eight in-
nings the score stands at eight to zip — in favor
of Pharaoh. Now, not only is Moses despised by
Pharaoh, but his own countrymen have had about
all they can take of him also.

Some mess!

Some failure!

Yet the story is not finished. There is still the
bottom of the ninth! There is still one more inning,
one more opportunity; and this is the one that a
sovereign God has been preparing His hard-working,
faithful servant for.

The Passover!

The Exodus!
Enter the Death Angel.
Exit the Children of Israel.

Israel is delivered from Egyptian bondage by a strong and mighty Arm, just as Moses had said. And the home run blast comes inevitable at the Red Sea, just so Pharaoh (or anybody else) would not have to doubt about the sudden success of this seeming failure.

You see, as Ethel Waters would often say, "Honey, Jesus don't sponsor no flops!"

Now, how about Peter? He serves as another example of the success of a great failure.

Peter is one of the original "open-mouth-insert-foot" type of guys. In his life we see the ups and downs that are so common to us all.

We see him one minute confessing great truths, and being told by Jesus, "Blessed are you, Simon" (Matthew 16:17), only to have him the next minute deny certain truths, and have the Lord rebuke him with an "Out of my sight, Satan!" (v.23).

Peter is impetuous, impulsive, brash, temperamental and scared. But — by the second chapter of Acts, Peter is the dominating force in the midst of the disciples. He is bold and decisive. He emerges as the leader of the early church.

He preaches one sermon, and three thousand people are saved! Now *that's* success! (Today we have to preach three thousand sermons to get one saved.)

Through Peter's ministry, people are healed, saved, baptized and added to the church. He is the most popular preacher around. He is in great demand, especially by the chief priests! Yet —

Their jails cannot hold him.
Their threats cannot intimidate him.
Their beatings cannot stop him.
A success? Absolutely.

But Peter, to this day, retains the distinction of having gone through one of the worst failings in Christianity.

He denied his Lord.

He swore he never knew Him!

He cursed and swore to prove it.

Imagine for a moment, if you will, how much he must have felt like a failure. What incredible emptiness he must have sensed in those moments following his convincing performance before the enemies of Christ! Imagine how cold and depressed his heart must have felt over against the warmth of the campfires of Christ's accusers.

He had failed!

Yet (and the point is) he went on to succeed. He became a success that in some regards may be unparalleled. Yes, Paul was a success, but in a different way. Abraham, David, the others — all successful — and yet it is Peter to whom we are most attracted. He is the one we are most at home with. He is the one we all identify with most closely. We can relate to him. He is the most like us!

History affords us other glimpses at great men who at times failed miserably, only to rebound in success. One thinks of the great composer George Frederic Handel, the man who gave us, among many brilliant works, perhaps the most famous religious oratorio of all time — the unparalleled *Messiah*.

Yet how many of us know that prior to the creation of *Messiah,* Handel had been reduced to poverty and bankruptcy. Although he tasted brief success, Handel nevertheless was forced to retire from public life a defeated man. He would wander despairingly along darkened London streets convinced he was without a friend anywhere in the world.

Added to this were various physical ailments. A cerebral hemorrhage paralyzed his right side.

He could hardly walk.

He could not move his right hand.

The doctors gave him no hope of recovering.

And then one night in total despair, he was confronted by an amateur poet named Charles Gibbon, who had a manuscript that he desired Handel to compose a score for. Remarkably, in just a matter of days, working feverishly in a little house, and rarely leaving his room, Handel composed the *Messiah* oratorio! It was performed first in Dublin in 1742, and is still enjoyed centuries later.

Success amid failure!

Another — the son of a poor preacher, the lowest in his college class, rejected from the ministry, a failure in both the legal and medical professions — he had to borrow clothes to wear. As a last desperate attempt to make a mark at anything, he started to write.

And write he did, and he became one of the greatest of all the eighteenth-century English poets, Oliver Goldsmith.

Another failure turned success, at age 53 had gone from one misfortune to another, one debt to another. His left hand was useless because of a war injury. He held several government jobs and failed at them all. He had even been in prison. Finally, he too picked up a pen and wrote a book that has thrilled the world for over three centuries. The failure — Cervantes. The success — *Don Quixote.*

How many of us know that one of the greatest of all American poets was for some twenty years a complete failure? He was thirty-nine before he ever sold a volume of poetry. Yet today Robert Frost is considered one of the finest writers ever. His poems have been published in some twenty-two languages. He won the Pulitzer Prize for poetry four times! He had more honorary degrees bestowed upon him than probably any other man of letters.

Seeming failures turned to incredible successes.

There is one more great illustration. Here is a man with less than one year of formal education as a child. In 1831 he fails miserably in business. Turning to politics, he is defeated in 1832 in a bid for a seat in his state's legislature. In 1833 in business, he again fails. Finally elected to the legislature in 1834, he suffers a nervous breakdown in 1836. He is defeated for Speaker in 1838; defeated for Elector in 1840; defeated for Congress in 1843, and again in 1848. He failed at an attempt to be elected to the Senate in 1854, and was defeated as a Vice-Presidential candidate in 1856. He was defeated for the Senate again in 1858.

This is the track record of a man who never stopped trying, even though his failures were many and his successes few. Here is a man who, today, remains one of the most revered and respected Americans in our country's history.

Here is a man who wrote, "God selects His own instruments, and sometimes they are queer ones; for instance, He chose me to steer the ship through a great crisis . . . and with His help I shall not fail."[1]

A failure? Yes, time and time again.

Defeated? Yes, but always to run again.

And run he did. For in 1860, Abraham Lincoln became America's sixteenth, and perhaps greatest President.

Again I repeat, "Success is nothing but failure wearing a fresh coat of paint." You may fail, but you can still succeed, and especially spiritually. God may have to take you through failure to get you ready for success.

And fail you will!

But succeed you will also — in, and for, Him.

Great men and women have proven it, time and time again, in their setbacks and in their successes.

Suggestions and Summary

- Before you resign ask God if it's His will that you be re-assigned. Your disappointment may be His appointment (Exodus 5:22 — 6:2; Acts 16:6-10).
- Stability means stay-ability! Don't give up on the tasks you believe important. Stick with it (1 Corinthians 15:58; Galatians 6:9).
- The successful accomplishment of anything comes by doing whatever has to be done, when it has to be done, in the way it ought to be done, whether you want to do it or not (Philippians 4:13,14; Hebrews 12:2).
- The key to benefiting from failure is not to allow it to stop you. Draw a ladder with a goal you want to accomplish at the top. Catalog in each rung both successes and failures in the process of attempting to reach that goal. Notice how these failures, as well as the successes, are intended to take you a step closer to your objective.

FIVE

THE BIG SUCCESS
OF THE LITTLE

THE *C* STUDENTS run the world!

At least that is what Harry Truman once said. It does remind me though of an interesting statement I heard once, that God is not looking for extraordinary men for ordinary work, but ordinary men for extraordinary work.

It would seem that many others agree in both secular and sacred fields.

For instance, John McKay, the renowned football coach, remarked that it is the average players who win most football games, and not the superstars.

Of course this seems to run contrary to everything else we are learning these days. The high pressure salesmen of success are quick to peddle the superstar complex. You just must be one, or else you're just not much.

With the possible exception of microchips and foreign cars, our culture has been led to believe that big is good and small is bad. The fact is, everything does not have to be big to be good!

Sad that, in our society, looks, surroundings and size are synonymous with success while things small, simple and ugly are not.

It would seem that Christians are recoiling under this unfair, as well as incorrect, ideology. Many Christians are reluctant to speak up if they sense that what they've got to say is not as awesome as the "celebrity" Christian with the polished testimony.

One day while walking to school with Charlie Brown and Linus, Lucy Van Pelt remembers that it is show-and-tell day at school. She asks Linus if he remembered to bring anything.

"Yes," Linus answers, "I have a couple of things here to show the class — " He then proceeds to unfold some papers. "These are copies I've been making of some of the Dead Sea Scrolls!"

Holding them up for Charlie Brown and Lucy to inspect, he continues, "This is a duplicate of a scroll of Isaiah chapters 38 to 40. It was made from seventeen pieces of sheepskin, and was found in a cave by a Bedouin shepherd."

Pulling out another, he says, "Here I've made a copy of the earliest known fragment ever found. It's a portion of 1 Samuel 23:9-16. I'll try to explain to the class how these manuscripts have influenced modern scholarship."

You can see the frustration building up on poor old Charlie Brown's face as Lucy responds, "Very interesting, Linus!"

Turning to Charlie Brown she asks, "And are you bringing something for show and tell, Charlie Brown?"

"Well," admits our dejected hero. "I had a little red fire engine here, but I think maybe I'll just forget it."

That's where many are in our churches today. All they've got is a little red fire truck, and they are convinced that it is not enough. Rather than speak, they remain silent. Instead of stepping out, rather than risk embarrassment, they stay home. What is a toy compared to the Dead Sea Scrolls anyway? How can a simple, quiet life given to the Lord in childhood years be as dynamic as the charismatic gunslinger who came to Christ out of a life of drugs, crime and fast-lane living? How can God use poor old Charlie Brown with his insignificant little red fire engine?

And yet God rarely works with the big, or the mighty, or the proud.

Francis of Assisi was once asked how he was able to accomplish so much. He answered, "Because the Lord looked down from Heaven and said, 'Where can I find the weakest, littlest man on earth?' Then He saw me and said, 'I've found him. I will work through him, and he won't be proud of it. He'll see that I am only using him because of his insignificance.' "

With inspired insight, the apostle Paul wrote to the Corinthian Christians, "Brothers, think of what you were when you were called. Not many of you were wise by human standards; not many were influential; not many were of noble birth. But God chose the foolish things of the world to shame the wise; God chose the weak things of the world to shame the strong. He chose the lowly things of this world and the despised things — and the things that are not — to nullify the things that are, so that no one may boast before Him" (1 Corinthians 1:26-29).

Incredible!

Confusing? Well, not really — at least not from God's viewpoint. Paul's last statement explains it. When all is said and done, and great jobs have been accomplished in spite of mean tools, God is the one who gets the glory!

Human sweat can add nothing to the Holy Spirit. God seeks to use that one humble person, filled with His Spirit, rather than that giant of a personality who would probably wind up stealing glory from God. The Scriptures are clear: No one may boast before Him.

There has been a little slogan going around that has attained a degree of popularity, but I believe it to be unscriptural: "It doesn't really matter who gets the credit, as long as God gets the glory." You see, the problem with a statement like that is that it betrays the pride of the human heart. The fact is that if anyone other than God gets the credit, it is unlikely that God will get the glory either.

Remember Gideon and his three hundred? Of course, he originally had a formidable force of some thirty-two thousand troops to take on the Midianites with.

Recall, further, how God whittled the army down twice, till all that remained were three hundred men. But why? Why not the larger force? I'm sure Gideon questioned God on this matter anxiously as the impending battle approached!

God answered.

"You have too many men for me to deliver Midian into their hands. In order that Israel may not boast against me that her own strength has saved her..." (Judges 7:2).

That's just like what Paul said!

That is the way God wants it, lest we pride ourselves in what we think we have accomplished. Lest, as mere flesh, we glory in His almighty presence. To insure that this comes to pass, God may even cause us to be little. He will even reduce us if need be "to show that this all-surpassing power is from God and not from us" (2 Corinthians 4:7).

> Great events we often find,
> On little things depend,
> And very small beginnings
> Have oft a mighty end.
> (Author Unknown)

We have to get over the mentality that success is gauged only by bigness. Why? Because there is a big success of the little. Subsequently, success stories have had humble beginnings.

Columbus was the son of a weaver, and a simple weaver himself. Homer was the son of a small farmer. Oliver Cromwell was the son of a London brewer. Benjamin Franklin was a journeyman printer. His father was a soapmaker. Shakespeare was the son of a stool stapler. Robert Burns was a simple plowman.

Simple roots. Small beginnings.

Someone commented that when God created man, He used dust, not uranium! When He spoke to Moses, He chose as a podium a small bush, not a mighty cedar. God's appreciation for the small and seemingly insignificant is documented time and time again in the Word of God. A poet described it thus:

> Shamgar had an ox-goad;
> Rahab had a string;
> Gideon had a trumpet;
> David had a sling;
> Samson had a jawbone;
> Moses had a rod;
> Dorcas had a needle —
> All were used for God.
> (Author Unknown)

While there is no limit to the success of the little, there is a key.

We must desire God to use us and enlarge whatever talent or gift He has granted us.

This great truth is seen again and again in the Word of God. Ordinary people, throughout the Bible, accomplishing great things for God even though their backgrounds were humble and crude. Men like Elisha, Amos, Jonah. Women like Ruth, Esther, Mary Magdalene.

They were all people just like us, really — simple folks never dreaming they would amount to anything, individuals who would triumph in the end, even though their beginnings seemed to be an end.

And yet that is God's style. He delights to use the meek and meager while He confounds the mighty.

He would rather choose a little lad with five small loaves and feed thousands (John 6:9) or pick a David with five stones to rule a nation (Psalm 119:41). He chose Bethlehem, in all its littleness, to bless the world (Micah 5:2).

No wonder the Word of God encourages us never to despise "the day of small things" (Zechariah 4:10).

If only we could appreciate how God truly values the little, how He delights to energize and enlarge upon it, how He wants to multiply it.

There does not seem to be much glory in His making a success out of the already "successful." He would rather confound the world by making a success out of the little.

Someone has well said that the person who is a Christian in small things is not a small Christian. It was Horatius Bonar who mentioned that the little things of the hour and not the great things of the age fill up a life.

So you're not a great athlete or a glamorous movie star or a dynamic political or community leader.

Perhaps your testimony does not include a deliverance from drugs, alcohol, communism or a cult.

No doubt your church does not occupy nor own a city block; few do.

The point is, God can still use you. And He would rather use the insignificant.

Jack Hyles, the well-known pastor of First Baptist Church of Hammond, Indiana, once told the story of being on a platform, early in his ministry, with some of the great preachers of the day. He was awed by their presence, and as a result of those humbling moments he later wrote these words:

> I'm just a little donkey
> Amidst stallions tall and white.
> They're each a gold talent
> And I, a widow's mite.
> I'm just a little pebble
> And each of them a stone;
> I'm a stunted bramble
> And they're trees — full grown.
> I'm just an unclean raven
> While they are nightingales;
> I am a little spinnow
> And they are mighty whales.
> I'm just a little sparrow,
> Yet they as eagles fly;
> I tip-toe through the tree tops
> While they soar through the sky.
> I'm just a little ox-goad
> And sharpened swords are they;
> While they are giant boulders,
> I'm just a piece of clay.
> I'm just a tiny flower,
> A lily in the field;
> I'm a little sling shot
> And they are mighty shields.
> Yet — God once used a donkey
> While stallions standed near;
> He tells us with the lily
> That He gives us what we wear.
> He used the dirty raven

To feed His prophet bread;
A little stone well chosen
To pierce Goliath's head.
He took a little sparrow
To show us of His care,
And used a mite, so tiny
To teach us how to share.
A little cactus bramble
Was king of all the trees;
He brought down with the sling-
     shot
The giant to his knees.
He made a worthy vessel
With one small piece of clay;
O, Mighty God of Mercy
Use me in power today!

Imagine — that God would use us in power. In all our smallness, in all our nothingness, in all our potential for failure. He can take sinful human beings and make them successful, consistent Christians.

He can employ our limited abilities and accomplish great and mighty things which we would never even have dreamed (Jeremiah 33:3).

To be sure, it makes no sense to the unregenerated world. However, our God believes that nothing succeeds like a desire to be used, no matter how "small" we may be.

There is indeed a big success of the little. Inversely, there is the little success of the big. I agree with Howard Hendricks when he says you may be at the top of the pile — but at the bottom of life. I think I would rather be in the company of Gideon, Columbus and Charlie Brown. How about you?

Suggestions and Summary

- Outward size is no indication of inward value (1 Samuel 16:7; Acts 12:21-23).
- A "big" person accomplishing a big task results in little glory for God. But a great God using a little person gets God all the glory (Judges 7:2; 2 Corinthians 4:7).
- There is a greater success with the little, as long as the little is given over to God (John 6:5-11; 1 Corinthians 2:4,5; Judges 3:31).
- In God's sight, it is not the amount but the motivation that counts. Look up the story of the widow's mite in Mark 12:41-44. Notice that Jesus was not sitting and watching how much people gave, but how they gave it (verse 41). Was the size of the gift important to Him? Whom did He commend?

SIX

SELF-DESTRUCTING SUCCESS

THERE IS A DANGER in success. George Bernard Shaw once admitted, "I dread success. To have succeeded is to have finished one's business on earth. I like a state of continual becoming, with a goal in front and not behind."

As odd as it may seem, success often comes equipped with its own self-destruct mechanism. Mentally, emotionally and spiritually there can be a tremendous letdown. It may even come as an unexpected interruption. In Luke 12, Jesus tells us of the story of a successful farmer. So successful was he that he decided to make some changes that would reflect his new status. He built greater barns to stockpile all his wealth. Then in utter satisfaction with his achievements, he kicked back and assumed an "eat, drink and be merry" attitude. The Lord concludes the story by showing God's displeasure at such a display of misplaced values. The rich farmer had become a misguided fool.

The very accomplishment and acknowledgement of his success was his downfall. He was sure he had made it, and therefore all that was left now was for him to enjoy it.

We can get like that. We get careless. We get self- sufficient. Confident that we are both the cause and effect, we sit back and enjoy the whole thing.

Churches on the whole can become like that one rich man. The ministry goes well, and God is blessing. There is a measure of success, and then certain things start to happen. Rather than staying on the cutting edge of meeting human needs, the church becomes self-centered. Maintaining takes the place of ministering. Budgets become more important than baptisms. Planning for new achievements gives way to parading old accomplishments. Creativity is overcome by mediocrity. The church, no longer hot, cannot even be cold — it just maintains room temperature.

Consider the Laodicean church in Revelation 3, a church merely enjoying its success. It was plagued with a smugness that led to lukewarmness. It gave up its first love in exchange for a bank account. Jesus' diagnosis of it is a stern indictment of the church today: "You say 'I am rich; I have acquired wealth, and do not need a thing.' But you do not realize you are wretched, pitiful, poor, blind, and naked" (Revelation 3:17).

What is it then, about success, that is so potentially dangerous? First of all, it must be that success brings satisfaction. Actually the danger is satisfaction with self, for self-satisfaction is the death of progress.

It is interesting to note that the apostle Paul was never satisfied. He pushed himself as well as others. He was perpetually motivated, always "straining toward what is ahead . . . pressing on toward the goal to win the prize for which God has called me heavenward" (Phillippians 3:13,14).

The Thessalonians were known all across the region for their working faith and their labor of love. Paul nevertheless exhorted them to work harder. The Philippians were known for their love of the brethren, and Paul further encouraged them to let their love abound even more. The Corinthians "came behind in no spiritual gift," and he clearly instructed them on how to use their gifts to an even greater extent for the glory of God.

Complacent? Never.

Settle in? Not a chance.

Become satisfied with a level attained? Not Paul. "Brothers, I do not consider yet to have taken hold of it . . . I press on" (Phillippians 3:13,14).

As someone has said, "The road to success is dotted with many tempting parking places." Paul rarely pulled over to park.

As an example of the premise of this chapter, I am challenged by the insight of John Wesley on the subject of revival. This founder of Methodism believed that every revival carried with it the seeds of its own declension. He wrote "I do not see how it is possible . . . for any revival to continue long. Religion must necessarily produce industry and these cannot but produce riches. As riches increase so will pride, anger and the love of the world."[1]

That, typically, brings us back full cycle to Revelation 3 and the rich, fat Laodicean Church.

Successful, and yet failing.

Church buildings filled with people who are not.

Bigger budgets yet less influence.

Increasing attendance yet decreasing commitment.

Big on creeds, little on deeds.

Self-satisfaction, however, is not the only danger in success, for another is self-sufficiency. A significant biblical example is Moses at the height of his ministry. The nation has been delivered from Egypt. The Ten Commandments have been given. Moses has spoken face to face with God. The Tabernacle, with all its glory, has been constructed. Manna from Heaven has fed the Israelites. They have drunk water from a rock. One crisis after another had been met head-on and dealt with successfully.

In the midst of all this success and satisfaction, Moses buckles under and gives way to the temptation to be something he's not. Although the meekest of men, he nevertheless commits a tragic blunder when he takes it upon himself to supersede (or at least reinterpret) God's instructions.

At Kadesh Barnea, instead of providing water for the children of Israel by simply speaking to the rock as God had commanded, Moses struck the rock — not once, but twice. The water came, and the people, as well as their animals, drank to the full, but Moses at the very peak of success self-destructed. His action was far reaching in that God forbade him the privilege of ever leading the children of Israel into the Land of Canaan. And why? The answer was not long in coming from God, "Because you did not trust in me enough to honor me as holy in the sight of the Israelites" (Numbers 20:12).

The implication is that Moses, in his disobedience, exalted himself in not exalting God. For one awful moment he failed to remember, as Paul would write centuries later, "Such confidence is ours through Christ before God. Not that we are competent to claim anything for ourselves, but our competence comes from God" (2 Corinthians 3:4,5).

There are so many other examples of the inherent danger in succeeding. Consider King David at the very pinnacle of his career. Instead of being on a battlefield with his army, his is on a rooftop with his lust. What follows unfortunately is a tragic chapter in an otherwise spotless career. A success story turned sour.

One of the Bible's greatest features is that it does not sugarcoat its heroes. We see them in their success, and we see them in their failure. The wisest man who ever lived got too smart for his own good (see Solomon). The strongest man who ever lived got too careless for his own good (see Samson). The big talker finally talks too much at the wrong campfire (see Peter). The man who stands head and shoulders above everybody else, nevertheless, gets jealous over a little-known shepherd boy (see King Saul).

While self-satisfaction and self-sufficiency are the two biggest factors in understanding success's failure, there are many more that are worthy of note.

A more modern term relating the danger of success is "burnout." The pressure to succeed in our society is great. We must succeed at all costs. Success at work is demanded, no matter how much stress the job brings. This striving for the top has therefore taken its toll.

Over 8 million Americans suffer with stomach ulcers.

Some 25 million Americans have high blood pressure.

More than 230 million prescriptions for tranquilizers are filled each year.

Another 12 million Americans are alcoholics.

The church is not exempt. Christians are suffering from burnout in record numbers. In an article entitled, "Burnout: The Risk of Reaching Too High," D. G. Kehl comments, "Christians are also particularly susceptible to burnout because of our typically idealistic/perfectionist aspirations and high expectations."[2]

Dr. Herbert J. Frendenberger, in his recent book, *Burn-out: The High Cost of High Achievement*, defined a burnout victim as "someone in a state of fatigue or frustration brought about by devotion to a cause, way of life, or relationship that failed to produce the expected reward."[3]

Now that may seem a little too psychoanalytic for some, but it tends to be quite descriptive of Moses (at Rephidim, Exodus 18:18), Elijah (under a juniper tree, 1 Kings 19), and Jonah (under a withering vine, Jonah 4).

Emotional burnout can be experienced by your teenagers because of the incredible peer pressures that they are subjected to. Men and women are succumbing to vocational burnout, as their jobs demand more of their time and energies. Husbands and wives give out and give up, and all because of an inability to meet each other's demands.

In church, we have been told for so long that we ought to boil over rather than fizzle out, that we have taken the advice literally. Boiling over may sound spiritual, but it's burnout just the same.

Jesus, however, offers a significant opportunity that addresses the issue. In Matthew 11:28-30, He gives an invitation to all the burned out, boiled over, fed up folks who are desperate in their situation. He says, "Come to me, all you who are weary and burdened, and I will give you rest . . . You will find rest for your souls."

As the Spirit of God has been given to be the "Comforter," literally the "Encourager," He is able to apply Jesus' offer directly to every believer. The Holy Spirit in filling us, controls us, and in controlling us, He contains us. The confusing frustration and fatigue is not stored or pent up, but it is transferred. Your life in exchange for His is the offer. Your turmoil for His tranquility. Your disorder for His direction. Hie peace for your perplexity (John 16:33).

Success can also bring along a sort of insensitivity with it. Prolonged success has a way of making us expect it always. One comes to accept as perfunctory the whole experience. Former Secretary of HEW John W. Gardiner once stated, "We succeed in one field of specialization and then become trapped in it. Nothing surprises us. We lose our sense of wonder."[4]

And then there is the possibility of selfishness. Success can cause one to become selfish. And yet success, to be real success, must be shared. Michel Quoist wrote, "Man cannot make a success of his life unless he is working to make a success of his world."[5]

There is one more potential failure in success that should be mentioned. That would be the tendency to overlook the smaller details of life.

At first this doesn't seem like any real threat. Yet, in the larger scope of attaining and maintaining success, oftentimes the littler and seemingly more unimportant items are ignored.

The Scriptures sufficiently warn us in this area. Solomon wrote, "The little foxes . . . ruin the vineyards" (Song of Solomon 2:15)..

Recently, I read an interesting story of the death of an enormous tree in Colorado. Such a large and aged tree it was that experts believe it must have been a seedling when Columbus discovered America. It was probably half grown when the pilgrims landed at Plymouth Rock.

It is said to have been struck by lightning some fourteen times. It survived centuries of Colorado's worst winters. Age never withered it. Avalanches could not move it. Fire did not destroy it.

But it was overcome, finally, by beetles! Little bugs so small that anyone could crush them between finger and thumb. And yet to the little, unobserved bug the mighty Colorado tree fell.[6]

> I thought, if defeat came at all,
> It would be in a big, bold
> Definite joust
> With a cause or a name.
> And it came.

I had not thought the daily skirmish
With a few details, worthwhile;
And so I turned my back upon them
Year on year; until one day
A million minutia blanketed together
Rose up and overwhelmed me.

(Author Unknown)

There are, then, these danger zones in success. There is in the process of succeeding the potential for real failure.

The ensuing self-satisfaction.

The inevitability of self-sufficiency.

The probability of burnout.

The dulling reality of insensitivity.

The possibility of selfishness.

The tendency to overlook smaller details.

These are what can sour any success. They can dampen and destroy any productive achievement. And the successful pursuit of any goal is too precious an accomplishment to have it fall victim to self-destruction, destruction that comes from within.

Suggestions and Summary

- Attempt to define the self-destructive tendencies in your own life. Sit down and objectively make a list of these characteristics. For example, can you admit pride? Do you become selfish when you receive or achieve something? On how many occasions have you become self-centered and insensitive to the needs of others? With list in hand, confess each one before the Father. In faith, transfer these burdens for God's peace.
- Write a paraphrase of Luke 12:16-21 by using your own name in place of the rich farmer. Fill in the other details as might pertain to your life, home, business, investments, and so on. How will the outcome read? Is there a need to re-prioritize these areas?
- The possibility of burnout at least admits the probability of fire. Seek to control the blaze (Ephesians 5:18).
- "Only virtue brings success worth having."[7]
- "The true way to be humble is not to stoop until you are smaller than yourself, but to stand at your real height against some higher Nature that will show you what the real smallness of your greatness is."[8]

SEVEN

STUMBLING BLOCKS OR STEPPING STONES

IN THE POPULAR CARTOON comic strip "Ziggy," there appeared the following scene: As our hero, Ziggy, in his little automobile, drove down a road, he saw two signs. The first read in big bold letters, "THE ROAD TO SUCCESS." Slightly down the road, though, stood the second sign, which read sympathetically, "PREPARE TO STOP FOR TOLLS."

The road to success is always paved with labor. There are tolls to be paid. And not only tolls, but there are toils also.

Problems to work around.

Hurdles to jump over.

Obstacles to push aside.

Like Ziggy, on the road to success we are confronted with the real possibility of failure and setbacks just around the corner.

In a previous chapter we were exposed to the example of many individuals who failed (and failed miserably), only to move on to great success.

What an encouragement to know that success can be ours in the midst of failure. Victory can be snatched from the jaws of defeat. You can still rise up when others are counting you down and out.

The obstacle that lies in your path may be the very platform upon which your faith can perform. This is not just positive-thinking propaganda, it is a recurring theme throughout the Bible. We are challenged continually to turn our stumbling blocks into stepping stones.

Our problem is that we would rather sidestep the issue. We would rather go around, under or over — anything but face the situation head-on and seek God's guidance in transforming a burden into a blessing.

It is a well established fact that many successful folks have become such even though they had to overcome various personal and physical handicaps.

Winston Churchill stuttered as a child (he flunked sixth grade) and still became one of this centuries greatest orators and statesmen.

Franklin D. Roosevelt was struck down as a child with infantile paralysis, and yet became the only man ever to be elected President of the United States for four terms.

Doctors told eight-year-old Glenn Cunningham, who was burned severely in a school fire, that he probably never would walk again. Instead, Glenn Cunningham became one of the great distance runners and set a world record in 1934 in the mile run.

Ludwig Von Beethoven was almost totally deaf before he reached his pinnacle as a composer.

How many know that John Milton was blind by age forty-four yet would go on to write *Paradise Lost?*

And what of John Bunyan, who would write the classic *Pilgrim's Progress* — from a prison cell?

Have we pondered someone like Fanny Crosby, who as a child was permanently blinded by a physician's blunder but went on to compose some of the greatest gospel hymns of all time? She said, "I believe that the greatest blessing the Creator ever bestowed on me was when He permitted my external vision to be closed. He consecrated me for the work for which He created me. I have never known what it was to see, and therefore I cannot realize my personal loss. But I have had the most remarkable dreams, I have seen the prettiest eyes, the most beautiful faces, the most remarkable landscapes. The loss of sight has been no loss to me."[1]

Max Cleland affords us a modern-day illustration. Losing both legs and an arm in Vietnam, he earned the admiration of all, rising to become head of the Veterans Administration in Washington, D.C.

God does not give us trials to make us bitter, but better; not to impair us, but to improve us; not for confinement, but for refinement. The psalmist says that the steps of a good man are ordered by the Lord, and George Mueller added that the "stops" as well as the steps are ordered.

It is an interesting study indeed to see how some biblical characters turned their stumbling blocks into stepping stones. Joseph stands out as the classic example. He was hated by his brothers and misunderstood by all around him. Literally sold into slavery, he eventually wound up in an Egyptian dungeon. Obstacles were all around him. And yet God had a plan.

Joseph was able to hurdle his obstacles to become second only to Pharaoh. It is not enough, however, to appreciate Joseph's rise to power in Egypt as a personal success story. It is not enough to think of his success in terms of what it did for him. His was a success story that benefited others, as all successes ought to.

Joseph, perhaps, knew this better than anyone else. He knew his success story was planned by God. Listen to his insight when finally a meeting between himself and his brothers, who had sold him into slavery years before, takes place: "But Joseph said to them, 'Don't be afraid. Am I in the place of God? You intended to harm me, but God intended it for good to accomplish what is now being done, the saving of many lives' " (Genesis 50:19,20).

It's as if he is saying, "You gave a stumbling block, but God turned it into a stepping stone." Indeed, it is the Romans 8:28 of the Old Testament. We must eventually come to learn also that all things work together for good to them that love God!

M. Mannington Dexter captures the beating heart of Joseph's faith:

> I knew I had been sold,
> For circumstance
> Dark as a desert pit
> And dismal as the slaver's caravan
> Surrounded me
> And seemed to crush me down.
> I had been sold.
> I also had been sent!
> The circumstance
> Shone with the night divine,
> And through the wrath of men
> God put me in His own appointed
>   place.
> He set on high
> And none could bow me down.
> I had been sent![2]

That's it! We always think in terms of being "sold," rarely of being "sent." We always complain that rosebushes have thorns, instead of praising God that thorn bushes have roses. We need Joseph's perspective to make our Christianity come alive once again.

Add to Joseph's experience those of Samson, Esther, Daniel and the apostle Paul, all of whom overcame obstacles and turned seeming failures into sterling successes in the Lord's work, and for His glory.

A further lesson that should be learned at this point is that all these people rarely lost sight of certain goals. They all believed that their personal mishaps could somehow become the ladder to success. Yet — and here's the important point — without exception, they agreed to allow God's Spirit to determine the outcome. Rather than being manipulative like so many of us, they waited on God, knowing that He is always on time.

They never lost a sense of purpose. Whether they were in an Egyptian pit, a lion's den, or a Roman prison. Their purpose, like ours should be, was to bring glory to God. Like them, we must place a higher priority on God's presence than on success.

Without God, no success is worth having. Without an abiding sense of Christ, joy departs. Not being filled, and thereby controlled, by the Holy Spirit, leaves a leanness of soul.

The most important thing about us should be not success attained, but fellowship with God maintained. That was more important to Jacob after one night of wrestling with the Lord than all his scheming and manipulating of other people before then.

It was more important to David than all the wealth and victories, praises of people, and beautiful Bathshebas. His earnest plea was, "Do not cast me from your presence or take your Holy Spirit from me" (Psalm 51:11).

Asaph was confused and somewhat bitter about the successes of the ungodly, until he was brought to see that the most profound truth concerning them is the void of their lives without God. His enlightened confession is, "Yet I am always with you" (Psalm 73:23).

After a career of many successes and few seeming failures, Solomon concludes, "Fear God and keep His commandments, for this is the whole duty of man" (Ecclesiastes 12:13).

The main thrust of the prophet Haggai's message was that the post-exilic Jews had built for themselves fine, paneled houses and respectable businesses, but in the process had forgotten God. No true success neglects God. They were sowing much but reaping little; eating but never being filled; dressing warmly but staying cold; and earning money only to put it into a purse with a hole in the bottom! (Haggai 1:6)

That is as fitting a commentary on our day as can be found in the Bible. It depicts people who are busy, but often busy about the wrong things. We are active, but our priorities betray all the energy expended as exercises in futility.

Someone has well said that you have removed most of the roadblocks to success when you have learned the difference between motion and direction.

We are good at motion, and emotion, and commotion, but it is purpose and direction that will help us turn those stumbling blocks into stepping stones. Quoist said it best: "Your limitations are not simply obstacles to your success; they are also indications from God of the path your life is to take."[3]

> Milton the blind, who looked on
> Paradise!
> Beethoven, deaf, who heard vast
> harmonies!
> Byron the lame, who climbed to-
> ward Alpine skies!
> Who pleads a handicap, remem-
> bering these?[4]

Suggestions and Summary

- All obstacles are opportunities to exercise faith (Genesis 50:19,20; Judges 16:21-31; Acts 28:30,31). List some of the obstacles you have encountered recently and consider how faith could have had a part in overcoming each one.
- Base your decisions not on your handicaps, but on God's promises (Exodus 4:10-12; 2 Corinthians 12:7-10; Romans 8:28).
- Success is a journey, not a destination. Seek God's plan for your life and keep moving! (Jeremiah 29:11; Psalm 73; Psalm 32:8; Job 23:10-14).
- "It's your attitude and not your aptitude that will determine your altitude."[5]
- Remember a kite rises highest AGAINST the wind, not with it (1 Peter 1:7; James 1:2-4).

> I cannot in the valley stay;
> The great horizons stretch away.
> The very cliffs that wall me round
> Are ladders unto higher ground!

EIGHT

THE GOD
OF THE VALLEYS

BENJAMIN DISRAELI once said that the most successful person in life is the one who has the best information. For the child of God, that means a knowledge of His Word. When all else fails — read the directions!

The pages of Scripture are full of principles and truths that are relevant to our study. One such example is found in 1 Kings 20.

Ben-Hadad, King of Aram, had gathered his enormous forces against Samaria. On the eve of the battle,, a prophet informed Ahab, King of Israel, that the nation would be spared, and that Ben-Hadad's army would be delivered into his hand.

As so it was, for with a great slaughter the Aramean army was defeated. In the retreat, Ben-Hadad is consoled by his servants: "Their [Israel's] gods are gods of the hills. That is why they were

too strong for us. But if we fight them on the plains,
surely we will be stronger than they" (1 Kings 20:23).

One can hardly blame the Aramean lieutenants
for seeking excuses for such a dismal defeat, yet
their reasoning strikes a divine nerve! It sets the
stage for the next confrontation one year later, as
we see in 1 Kings 20:26-29:

> The next spring Ben-Hadad mustered the
> Arameans and went up to Aphek to fight
> against Israel. When the Israelites were also
> mustered and given provisions, they marched
> out to meet them. The Israelites camped oppo-
> site them like two small flocks of goats, while
> the Arameans covered the countryside.
>
> The man of God came up and told the king
> of Israel, "This is what the LORD says: 'Because
> the Arameans think the LORD is a god of the
> hills and not a god of the valleys, I will deliver
> this vast army into your hands, and you will
> know that I am the LORD.' "
>
> For seven days they camped opposite each
> other, and on the seventh day the battle was
> joined. The Israelites inflicted a hundred
> thousand casualties on the Aramean foot sol-
> diers in one day.

Incredible! The Lord had not forgotten the challenge inadvertently offered a year earlier. The
gauntlet had been thrown down and God picked it
up. God's providential ability was on the line. His
might and strategy were called into question. Our
God waited a year to prove that He was not just
"a god of the hills," as the Arameans had thought,
but that He was also "a god of the valleys!"

There has always been a belief in the world
that would parallel that of the Arameans. But the
sad fact is that it has now become the mentality of
many in Christianity. It is the attitude that if some-

thing is good, it's from God, and if it is bad, it's from the devil.

Success implies God's blessings, while failure betrays God's disapproval, displeasure, or disinterest.

A mountaintop experience means God is with us, while a valley experience means we've been all but forsaken and we're on our own. Hence we attempt to skip from one mountaintop high to another, only to land painfully in some valley.

A business deal falls through to your dismay, and to the delight of a snickering rival. Thud! You hit the valley of humiliation.

Your teenage daughter, in anguish, informs you that she is pregnant. Frustration and hurt rise up around you like mountains, and you're left in the valley of despair.

A project you've been working on is rejected, or special friends you can't imagine being without move away, or the romance in your marriage is all but gone, or sickness burdens the family, or there's no more money, or — just a multitude of other things, all of which drive us into a valley of depression. *Is God there too?* We wonder.

Can we really count on His Spirit to be the divine Comforter, as He is so frequently called in the New Testament? Will He be there? Will He come alongside and console? Will the valley seem bearable if the Lord shares our yoke? Is He angry with us for being down in the pits in the first place? And will He leave us there to teach us a good lesson in the second place?

It's at those times that we must remember the message of 1 Kings 20 — that our God is not just God of the hills, but He is also God of the valleys. We must not fail to see that for us, as with Israel, there are victories to be won down in the pits!

The Bible makes it clear that there is a value to the valleys. Rightly identifying valley experiences as growth-producing times of trial and testing, hear-tache and failure, it's not hard to understand the Lord's purpose for them.

> I walked a mile with pleasure;
> She chatted all the way,
> But left me none the wiser
> For all she had to say.
>
> I walked a mile with sorrow
> And never a word spake she;
> But oh the things I learned
> When sorrow walked with me.[1]

As the writer of Hebrews informs us, no time of testing is joyous, nevertheless God not only allows, but in fact, also causes these times to enter our lives (Hebrews 12:11).

That is a threatening concept to some. They argue that God would never directly *cause* anything negative to happen to His child. He *allows* trials, they claim, but surely He never causes them.

Of course that is simplistic theology fueled by the success-prone mentality of our society. It never takes the time to consider the deeper reasons for God's actions. It has overlooked such clear statements as:

> But though he cause grief, yet will he have compassion according to the multitude of his mercies (Lamentations 3:3, KJV).
>
> See now that I, even I, am he, and there is no god with me: I kill, and I make alive; I wound, and I heal: neither is there any that can deliver out of my hand (Deuteronomy 32:39, KJV).
>
> Come, let us return to the Lord. He has torn us to pieces, but he will heal us; he has injured us but he will bind up our wounds (Hosea 6:1).

No doubt Job said it best, when to his wife he declared, "Shall we accept good from God, and not trouble?" (Job 2:10).

C. S. Lewis once observed that we really do not want a Father in heaven as much as a Grandfather in heaven, whose ultimate plan for everyone is such that it might be said at the close of each day that a good time was had by all.

We must come to learn that there is a real value to failure, to suffering and to trials. There is much to be learned as you hike through a valley.

Christlikeness is one lesson that should be learned. As we suffer we learn what it is like to be more like Him who suffered for us. Hence Paul would yearn to know "the fellowship of sharing in his sufferings" (Philippians 3:10).

Peter exhorts that we rejoice in manifold temptations, so that through testing, our faith might be praiseworthy at the coming of Christ (1 Peter 1:6,7).

James, likewise, instructs us that the trying of our faith works patience into our lives, a patience that leaves us whole, lacking nothing (James 1:2-4).

A value of the valley is that it causes us to listen better for God. God would like to speak to us during times of prosperity, but He always seems to have a better audience during times of adversity.

After a violent thunderstorm during a PGA tournament, golfer Lee Trevino was asked what he thought about when lightning struck a tree very near to where he was standing. "I learned," Trevino gulped, "that when God wants to play through, you had better let Him!"

Now that's a refreshing approach to the problem! God uses trials to get our attention. He has something to say, and we had better give an ear. There seems to be no doubt that we'll get a far better education in the valley. There we'll learn things that cannot be understood anywhere else.

Some time ago gospel song writer Andrae Crouch put it this way: "I thank God for the mountains/ and I thank Him for the valleys/ I thank Him for the storms He brought me through./ For if I'd never had a problem,/ I wouldn't know that He could solve them,/ I'd never know what faith in God could do."[2]

That is the value of the valley. The success merchants demand the mountains, for only there will God meet with us, we're told. And yet, our God is God of the valleys too, and He is pleased to be with us there and teach us along the way. We need the valleys.

We need them not only for the lessons they teach us, but also for the successes they lead to. There is a victory in the valley, no matter what type of valley it may be. The Bible mentions more than thirty, many of which become deep pools of devotional truth. Consider, for instance, the most well-known valley in the Bible, "the valley of the shadow of death," mentioned in the Twenty-Third Psalm.

Although this particular psalm has often been confined to funeral homes, dying and going to heaven is not its theme, but rather living victoriously on earth.

The valley of death and dying (literally "a canopy of curruption") is all around us, yet the acknowledgement is that "I will fear no evil, for you are with me."

The Shepherd's Psalm is a promise like no other that God is going to maintain His presence with me through all occasions of life. Shall we not take comfort in that? His is a promise to get me through the valleys of potential failure and pain during my lifetime. A table, I am told, is set up for me in the very face of my enemies (proof, by the way, that the message of the Twenty-Third Psalm is for protection on earth and not passage into heaven, unless, of course, you're expecting to find enemies in heaven).

We are promised not only His own presence, but His own very special escorts — goodness and mercy. And all that in the valley!

Perhaps your valley is as in Psalm 84:5,6 — the "Valley of Baca." Baca means "weeping," and one is reminded of Tozer's statement that it is doubtful whether God can bless a man greatly until He has hurt Him deeply.

Yet even here, the Scripture implies that you can turn your weeping into a well; your malady into melody; your stumbling blocks into stepping stones. As a pit fills up with rainwater, you can simply rise up and float out!

Perhaps your valley is the "Valley of Achor," the valley of trouble, or disturbance. It is there where Achan was found guilty of troubling Israel and stoned to death (Joshua 7:25,26).

But it is also there that God declared He would cause the valley to be a place where flocks would lie down in peace (Isaiah 65:10). He would turn trouble into triumph. Hosea identified Achor as "a door of hope" (Hosea 2:15).

I repeat, there is a victory to be had in the valley:
life over death,
joy over tears,
triumph over trouble,
melody over malady.

When we despise the valley, we make the same costly mistake the Arameans did centuries ago. When we fail to realize that our God is able to take us on to victory even through the deep valleys of our lives, we miss out on some of the most precious blessings He has in store for us.

Do not overlook the valleys!

Do not despise trials, tribulation and failure.

Frustration is often the way to triumph. Tribulation's imprint is on all great things. Crowns are cast in crucibles. As someone observed, scars are the price of scepters, and grief has always been the lot of greatness.

> Looking back it seems to me
> All the griefs which had to be
> Left me, when the pain was o'er,
> Richer than I'd been before;
> And by every hurt and blow
> Suffered in the Long-ago,
> I can face the world today
> In a bigger, kindlier way.
> Pleasure doesn't make the man,
> Life requires a sterner plan.
> He who never knows a care
> Never learns what he can bear.
> (Author unkown)

Suggestions and Summary

- Study the ups and downs of the children of Israel in the Old Testament, especially in the book of Judges. Catalog the principles of obedience, courage and faith. Seek ways to make application to your own life (1 Corinthians 10:11; Romans 15:4).
- Remember that produce is grown down in the valley, not on the mountain top. List the things you've learned, and how you've grown during times of trial (1 Corinthians 10:13; James 1:2-5; Hebrews 12:11-14).
- Memorize the Twenty-Third Psalm. Seek to apply its wonderful truths to the living of your life every day, rather than storing it us for your death someday. Consider:

The Author of Victorious Living ..... verse 1
The Atmosphere of Victorious
Living .... verse 2
The Appropriation of Victorious
Living .... verse 3
The Acknowledgement of Victorious
Living .... verse 4
The Abundance of Victorious
Living .... verse 5
The Assurance of Victorious
Living .... verse 6

NINE

IN THE SCHOOL OF FAILURE

THERE IS THE STORY of the young executive who, in seeking advice from a gray-haired colleague, asked, "Can you tell me what has been the secret of your success?"

"The secret, friend, is two words: right decisions!" replied the older man.

"But how do you make right decisions?"

"One word," came the answer, "experience."

"But how do you get experience?"

The old man smiled, "Two words: wrong decisions!"

There are some things that we will come to learn after we think we know it all. For instance we need to appreciate once and for all that we can learn from failure. Unfortunately, the only thing most people learn in failing is how to blame it on someone else. It's like an old sage once observed, "The man who can smile when things go wrong has thought of someone he can blame it on."

In a lot of ways, we have become a country of cop-outs, a nation of nit-pickers and fault-finders. The Executive branch blames the Congress, and Congress blames the Judiciary. State officials blame the county, and county officials blame the Federal Government. Students blame teachers, and teachers blame parents. Parishioners blame pastors, and the pastors blame the seminaries. It becomes one endless passing of the proverbial buck, ad nauseam.

Failure is, however, an important schoolroom in life's education. It was Emerson who said that bad times have a scientific value, and that these are occasions that a good learner will not miss. For some reason, though, we would rather graduate without ever having to endure exams.

We want to win the war without fighting any battles.

We want to ascend the ladder of success without slipping through the rungs.

Yet a flunked exam makes us study harder for the next test. And a lost battle makes us prepare harder for the next fight. And a slip makes us watch our step a little more closely the next time up.

As one editorialist stated, failures at random may help us learn about life in general.

It is quite clear, however, that failure is one school from which we would rather be truant. Subsequently, we are ill-prepared for failure. We rarely are taught to expect it, or most importantly, to learn from it.

J. Wallace Hamilton informs us that:

> The increase of suicides, alcoholics, and even some forms of nervous breakdowns is evidence that many people are training for success when they should be training for failure. Failure is far more common than success; poverty is more

prevalent than wealth, and disappointment more normal than arrival.[1]

Rarely learning valuable lessons from setbacks, we have burned out in our hot pursuit of succeeding at all costs.

Learning from my failures means that I am in fact a success in the school of failure. Shall we not then consider this more valuable than being, on the other hand, a failure in the school of success?

William Marston wrote, "If there is any single factor that makes for success in living, it is the ability to draw dividends from defeat.[2]

Dave Breese suggests that we need to learn how to renew our strength by enjoying partial successes. "Consider, if you will," he says, "that the recognition of an unsolved problem is not necessarily the recognition of failure but just may be the necessary first step in eventual success."[3]

It is said that Thomas Edison admitted to experiencing some six hundred failures before he finally perfected the incandescent bulb. One acquaintance remarked, "Six hundred failures, Mr. Edison! Weren't you discouraged?"

"Discouraged?" replied the great inventor. "Young man, I learned at least one lesson from every failure. What more could you ask?"

As we have seen, the Scriptures tell of many who went through the school of failure — and learned their lessons well. From Jonah to Peter, the class rolls swell. Perhaps the clearest picture, though, is a student named Samson.

You will recall that Judges 13 through 16 comprise the semesters of Samson's life. By Judges 16, he was a total failure. His eyes blinded, his reputation shot, his freedom was gone.

Through his own folly and lust he fell into the hands of his enemies. Delilah cut his hair, the

Philistines gouged out his eyes and the masses laughed him to scorn.

Instead of delivering Israel as a Judge, he ground grain in prison chains. He became a slave to pagans. Where once the Spirit of God moved him, he was now made sport of by idolaters. He had failed himself, his family, his nation, and most of all, his God!

But there would be one more exam before Graduation Day! And one has to wonder how much "study time" Samson put in as he stumbled around the grain in fetters of brass.

How he must have retraced the steps that led to his downfall! Surely he recalled how God had used him in the past. He had been a shining success story to a nation sorely lacking in heroes. And no doubt, at some time down in that dark, dingy dungeon, he told God that he had learned his lesson. If God would give him one more shot, he would not fail Him again.

Well, Graduation Day arrived, in the form of a big, idolatrous bash for the fish god, Dagon. The arena was packed with Philistines, and from the prison house Samson was led out to be made sport of. Little did the lords of the five cities know that Jehovah was preparing His student's test paper, and that Samson was about to fill it out with their blood.

As he was chained to the supporting pillars, the student in the school of failure lifted up his voice to Heaven: "O Sovereign Lord, remember me. O God, please strengthen me just once more, and let me with one blow get revenge on the Philistines for my two eyes" (Judges 16:28).

It's as if he cried, "I have known how to fail — now help me to succeed in the very midst of my failure."

And succeed he did! With his Nazarite locks flowing once again, and the Spirit of God strengthening him as of old, Samson dislodged the pillars and caused the entire pagan arena to collapse upon the Philistines. In the context of the history of his career, the success is calculated in Scriptures with the record that "the dead which he slew at his death were more than they which he slew in his life" (Judges 16:30, KJV).

His body was returned to Israel with honor. His memory made his brethren proud. His reputation was redeemed. His work was accomplished. He learned his lesson in the school of failure, and he ultimately graduated a success!

> Have you missed in your aim?
>   Well, the mark is still shining.
> Did you faint in the race?
>   Well, take breath for the next.
> Did the clouds drive you back?
>   But see yonder their lining.
> Were you tempted and fell?
>   Let it serve for a text.
> As each year hurries by let it join that procession
>   Of skeleton shapes that march down to the past,
> While you take your place in the line of progression,
>   With your eyes on the heavens, your face to the blast.
> I tell you the future can hold no terrors
>   For any sad soul while the stars revolve,
> If he will stand firm on the grave of his errors,
>   And instead of regretting, resolve, resolve.[4]

"A man's success is made up of failures," Ralph Waldo Emerson once said, "because he experiments and ventures every day, and the more falls he gets, moves faster on."[5]

Failing in one course may cause you to change your major to another. Certain setbacks can actually lead you to succeed in other areas.

Occasionally you may even think you have failed, when perhaps you have really succeeded in another area that you are simply blinded to. A certain comic strip illustrated the point in depicting a cave-

man standing inside his cave next to a small fir, a
crude wheel, a spear and a hatchet. Somewhat dejectedly he remarks to a visiting caveman, "So far,
none of them is a telephone, but I'll keep trying!"

That's the School of Failure.

It makes the man, it makes the woman. There
is no other school quite like it. Ask anyone from
Samson to David, from Solomon to Jonah, from
Edison to the wise old executive with whom we
began this chapter.

They, along with a host of others, will tell you
that failure's lessons are invaluable. They are the
tough exams that go to make up a successful graduation. We should use failures as stepping stones
rather than allow them to become stumbling blocks.
We must study

and learn,

and prepare,

and try again!

Only where there are graves can there be resur-
rections.

Suggestions and Summary

- Do not blame your failings on someone else. Lay your failure down at the throne of God, rather than at the doorstep of a friend (Genesis 3:(9-14; Hebrews 4:16).
- Do not look for an *excuse* for your failure, rather, seek a *use* for your failure.
- Refer to your list of some of your most recent setbacks. How might each one be useful to you — perhaps in a different way, or in another area?
- All immediate failures can lead to eventual successes, perhaps in other areas. Allow failures to suggest alternatives. Follow through on these.

TEN

FREEDOM TO FAIL, FAITH TO SUCCEED

"IF ANY ASKS what prospect of ultimate success, tell them, as much as there is an almighty and faithful God, Who will perform His promises, and no more."

Such were the words of the great Baptist missionary, Adoniram Judson, in response to those who were criticizing his work in Burma — work that after six years had failed to produce even one convert.

Judson had faith to succeed, however, and succeed he would! It is said that at his death in 1850, he left behind him in Burma 7,000 Christians, 63 churches and 163 missionaries. To this, add the fact that he wrote a Burmese grammar, a Burmese dictionary and translated the Bible into Burmese.

I believe the intriguing thing about the great missionary's words, though, is that they not only suggest a faith to believe God for success, but that they seem to demand a freedom to fail! Not swayed by outside opinion or statistics, and believing in the God who had called him to his mission field, Judson demanded that success or failure were totally up to the sovereignty of God. As much, therefore, as God would have the work succeed, it would!

An attitude such as this, of a freedom to fail, yet a faith to succeed, is desperately needed in the church today.

We need some space.

We need the time to work things out.

We need a faith to face failure, and a freedom to work it into success.

We must have the occasion to sift through the wood, hay and stubble for the precious stones, gold and silver.

At the 1977 commencement service of Gordon College, Dr. Vernon Grounds, then president of Conservative Baptist Theological Seminary in Denver, Colorado, spoke on this very subject as he addressed the graduation class on "Faith For Failure." Such a stimulating perspective was it, that *Christianity Today* decided to publish it that same year. In that address, Dr. Grounds shared such sound insights as:

> Our colleges and seminaries are unwittingly inoculating students with the virus of worldly success....Maybe we have been failing to communicate a cleancut Biblical understanding of success. And...therefore, we fail to prepare our graduates for an experience of failure which from God's standpoint is praiseworthy success.[1]

Then after making the observation that as the world judges success, the majority of those graduating seniors would be failures, Dr. Grounds nevertheless asked pointedly,

> Do you have the faith to hang onto principles of success despite worldly failure? Do you have the faith to keep doing God's will even if you

are unappreciated, unsung and unapplauded?
Do you have the faith to face failure?[2]

Jesus gave His disciples the space they needed
to work out His great challenges. He gave them
freedom to fail, and then, when they did, He instructed them further. He taught with repetition,
tapping into their need to have their faith
strengthened.

The church must do likewise. We must encour-
age faith through failure. Somehow we have to give
people a chance to work out what they believe God
has worked in. Our churches are usually not charac-
terized by freedom in this way, but rather by profes-
sionalism that demands perfection. Like Job's three
"friends," our counsel is that failure is a sure sign
of God's displeasure and judgment. Success, on the
other hand, is proof positive that you are highly
favored.

A. W. Tozer remarked that "God will allow His
servant to succeed when he has learned that success
does not make him dearer to God nor more valuable
in the total scheme of things."[3]

How we have missed that! In our push for
success we have forgotten how God's favor can really
be secured.

Not with crowds or converts, as Tozer would
warn us.

Not with the size of sanctuaries, salaries or
Sunday schools, as Grounds would alert us.

But by *faith!*

Listen again to the writer of Hebrews: "Without
faith it is impossible to please God"(Hebrews 11:6).

The enemy of our souls knows that it is by
faith that we draw nearer to our God. The devil
knows better than we that doubt is practical atheism.

If he can incite us to doubt, to worry, to fret,
to complain, to disbelieve, he has accomplished a

major task in his program to bring a wedge between
ourselves and the Lord God.

Although the devil's design is that we give up,
we can go on! He would have us run and hide, but
we can stand up and fight! He wants us to murmur
and complain, but we can believe and pray! He
wants us whining; God wants us winning!

We can hang our heads and moan and weep
or, like Paul and Silus, we can turn our deep, dark,
dank dungeon into a platform of prayer and praise.
As someone aptly wrote:

> Oh let us rejoice in the Lord ever-
>   more
> When doubts of the tempter
>   are flying,
> For Satan still dreads, as he oft
>   did of yore
> Our singing much more than
>   our sighing.
>   (Author unknown)

We need spiritual optimism, an optimism that
requires an almost reckless freedom to explore and
experiment, and expect great things from God.

Is there room in your house for failure? Does
your son know that he has the freedom to develop,
and that faith in God is the basis for his succeeding?
Can the shattered dream of your broken-hearted
teenager be reconstructed as you share with her that
God still has a plan for her life? A failure, any failure,
has not changed that, if only she will believe.

Faith indeed is victory that overcomes. Are we
willing to give other people a chance to exercise it?
Unfortunately, the drawback to our exerting faith is
our own willingness to doubt. If we can't win, we
can always worry.

Paul Adolph wrote that "anxiety and worry
represent forms of fear which project themselves

with imaginary situations which never come to pass."[4]

Worry, we have been told, will give us something to do, but never get us anywhere. Worry is interest paid on trouble before it falls due. Worry is unbelief parading around in disguise!

Perhaps nothing grieves the Spirit of God more than the manifestation of doubt and unbelief in our lives. Scripture is clear in encouraging us that faith unlocks God's great resource. He delights to respond to the one who will but believe in His promises and take Him at His Word.

On the other hand, we are shown also that unbelief is the surest way of disenfranchising ourselves from God's actions. Jesus refused to do any mighty works in Nazareth. Why? Because of their unbelief (Matthew 13:58).

The Lord confronted unbelief in the lives of the disciples every time it manifested itself. He showed them repeatedly that, at best, it was a denial of God's revelation to them. To doubt was to deny God's Word.

A classic example of this takes place during one of the occasions when Jesus and the disciples had to cross the Sea of Galilee. While they were out on the sea, a terrific storm came up. The disciples, mostly fishermen, mind you, were scared to death, and finally they woke up the Lord, who had fallen asleep in the bow of the boat.

They were sure that destruction was imminent. Any minute the boat would capsize, or break apart, and they would all perish in the violent waters. Jesus stood, rebuked the raging wind and water, and then in the ensuing calmness turned to the disciples and asked, "Where is your faith?" (Luke 8:25).

Faith? Now that does not seem to be a fair question. Why did He question their faith? Why

didn't He ask who was handling the helm, or man-
ning the oars, or bailing the water? The answer lies
in the fact that He knew what their problem was.
They needed a lesson, not in seamanship, but in
taking God at His Word. Remember, Jesus had said
when they got into the boat, "Let's go over to the
other side of the lake." They should have remembered that He had said, "Let's go over," and nothing
about under! (Luke 8:22-25).

Unbelief does that to us. We somehow forget
what God says. Subsequently, without God's Word
we self-destruct. We pay an awful price. Friedrich
Krummacher wrote, "Unbelief does nothing but dar-
ken and destroy. It makes the world a moral desert,
where no divine footsteps are heard."[5] Thomas Car-
lyle wrote, "There is but one thing without honor,
smitten with eternal barrenness and an inability to
do or to be, and that is unbelief."[6] Meeler Markham
said, "Doubt has been a deterrent to progress, a
danger to institutions, and a destroyer of the good
things of life. Doubt comes as a hanger of crepe in
the hall of joy, as an idler of hands in a busy work-
shop, as a robber of the fullness of life, as a poisoner
of minds, a blighter of hopes, [and] a paralyzer of
effort."[7]

No wonder unbelief grieves the Spirit. Jesus
marveled at it (Mark 6:6). It is a slap at divinity. It is
a refusal of providence, a rejection of God's promises.

Imagine if your children, through word and
action, denied your ability to work and provide for
them. How would you feel if your little son or
daughter came right out and told you that they did
not have confidence in you as their father? Perhaps
they would question whether you were strong
enough to protect them, or wise enough to direct
them, or loving enough to care for them. Your heart
would break.

God the Father has promised His children all that and more. In Christ, He has provided us perfect redemption. Through His Spirit, we have His abiding presence. Paul tells us that we are complete in Him (Colossians 2:10). How His heart must break when we deny it all through unbelief!

Faith is always the cure for fear. Believing in God's promises is always the antidote to worry and doubt. This type of faith brings a freedom to act. We need the faith that has its eye on God rather than on circumstance. George Mueller's observation is timeless. The captain of a fogbound liner protested when he requested that the ship proceed to their destination. "The fog is too dense," he warned. Having just prayed, Mr. Mueller responded, "My eye is not on the density of the fog."

What God expects from us is faith for today — belief in His providence just for today, rather than anxiety in the failures of yesterday, or the fears of tomorrow. It is sad that today's happiness is often crucified between two thieves — yesterday's misery and tomorrow's anxiety.

A freedom to fail and a faith to succeed does not concern itself with fretting about the past or worrying about the future. It knows nothing of the attitude set forth by the fellow who was asked by an acquaintance, "What are you thinking of, my friend? You look so depressed."

"My future," came the reply.

"Well, what makes it look so hopeless and dismal?"

"My past."

> Stand out in the sunlight of Prom-
> ise, forgetting
> Whatever the Past held of sor-
> row or wrong.

We waste half our strength in a
useless regretting;
We sit by old tombs in the dark
too long.

(Author unknown)

A freedom to fail is not to feel the weight of
peer pressure or the burden of critics with their
statistics.

Imagine what the critics must have said about
Abraham or written about Noah. Not much to show,
initially, for years of toil, yet they believed God and
continued to work on. They, like hundreds of others,
had a freedom and a faith to keep at it in light of
and in spite of seeming futility and failure. One
overriding motivation pushed them. Like Moses,
Nehemiah, David, Paul, and a host of others, the
"one thing" (Philippians 3:13) was to forget about
past failures or successes and push on to please God
rather than man.

Clovis Chappell told of walking into a newspaper office and seeing a large sign on the wall: "57
RULES FOR MAKING A SUCCESS." Dr. Chappell
thought to himself, "Here is where I tarry. With
fifty-seven fingers pointing the way to success, even
I need not miss it." He walked closer, and read the
rules as follows: "Rule number one: DELIVER THE
GOODS. Rule number two: It doesn't matter about
the other fifty-six!"[8]

That's it! Forget about all the success manuals;
just set your heart on laboring hard for God.

Deliver the goods.

Let God work out the results.

A freedom to fail, then, is to learn better God's
program of faith. Furthermore, a faith to succeed is
to know full well that where God guides, He provides, and that all such success is squarely His
responsibility.

What simplicity! What freedom!

Suggestions and Summary

- "The man who is elated by success and cast down by failure is still a carnal man."[9]
- Learn to trust God even though you cannot trace Him (Hebrews 11:1-6; Mark 11:22; Psalm 37:5).
- List the things that cause anxiety in your life (the things that cause you to worry). Find a promise in God's Word that addresses each one. For instance:

> Finances .... Philippians 4:19
> Sickness ... 1 Corinthians 10:13
> Employment .... Psalm 37:25
> Children .... Proverbs 22:6

- "I would rather fail in the cause that someday will triumph than triumph in a cause that someday will fail."[10]

ELEVEN

CHEER UP!
THE WORST
IS YET TO COME

I AM AN OPTIMIST. An optimist is someone who sees an opportunity in every problem, while a pessimist sees a problem in every opportunity. For me, then, writing this chapter is a delight.

The Bible has both optimists and pessimists within its pages. Abraham was an optimist, King Saul a pessimist. David was an optimist, Moses, at times was a pessimist. Nehemiah was an optimist, Jeremiah a pessimist. One of the greatest optimists was Joseph in the Old Testament. Some of the greatest pessimists were Job's friends, Eliphaz, Bildad and Zophar. Paul was an optimist, and of course, so was Jesus.

The child of God ought to be optimistic, in that the Word of God has revealed to us God's game plan. We've won! No matter how weird it gets, we are on the winning side. We can afford to be enthusiastically optimistic, even when it seems like the world is going to cave in around us. And it might.

Prophecy underscores the fact that dark days lie ahead. The apocalyptic message is that it is going to get worse before it gets better. Although paradoxical, the advice to Christians is, "Cheer up — the worst is yet to come."

This type of philosophy of living is what Romans 8:28 is all about: "And we know that in all things God works for the good of those who love him, who have been called according to His purpose." It is what prompted Paul to tell the Corinthians, "For our light affliction, which is but for a moment, worketh for us a far more exceeding and eternal weight of glory (2 Corinthians 4:17, KJV). It is what helped Peter to exhort the early Christians during the awful years of persecution under Nero, "But rejoice that you participate in the sufferings of Christ, so that you may be overjoyed when His glory is revealed" (1 Peter 4:13).

Christians are to live a lifestyle that is a paradox. A.W. Tozer perhaps summed it up best when he wrote that a Christian "feels supreme love for One whom he has never seen, talks familiarly every day to Someone he cannot see, expects to go to heaven on the virtue of Another, empties himself in order to be full, admits he is wrong so he can be declared right, goes down in order to get up, is strongest when he is weakest, richest when he is poorest, and happiest when he feels worst. He dies so he can live, forsakes in order to have, gives away so he can keep, sees the invisible, hears the inaudible, and knows that which passeth knowledge. And all the while he may be confounding his critics by his unbelievable practicality."[1]

The ability to live this way comes from the presence of the Spirit of God. It is a tough lifestyle, that only gets tougher, and the power to live it at all comes from the indwelling Holy Spirit. We have this power in "earthen vessels," so that when someone views our resource and resilience, he is bound to give God the credit and not us (2 Corinthians 4:7).

This type of paradoxical living is clearly spelled out in 2 Corinthians 4:7-11. In a masterful series of word plays, Paul outlines the ideal Christian optimism. He says first of all that we are "troubled on every side, yet not distressed." The word he uses for "trouble" means to be crowded, or to be pressed upon. It is the same word Peter used in answering the Lord in Luke 8:45, where in the midst of a crowd Jesus asked, "Who touched me?" Peter, somewhat amazed, responded that the multitude thronged and pressed Him. That's the picture Paul draws — of those times in life when we feel crowded and closed in upon, those stifling times, when we gasp for air, feeling that we will suffocate at any minute.

Paul knew those times. He admitted to the Corinthians that "when we were come into Macedonia, our flesh had no rest, but we were troubled [same word] on every side; without were fightings, within were fears" (2 Corinthians 7:5, KJV). Most of us can identify with that. The pressures of life squeeze down like a vice. They become almost unbearable. And yet Paul says that we are not distressed. Here the word he uses means narrowness of place, from a word meaning literally "to hem something in." While we admit to being pressed down, we affirm we are never hemmed in.

He continues by saying that we are "perplexed, but not in despair." The words "perplexed" and "despair" are taken from the same basic root word in Greek, a word meaning "travel," or "way." Paul prefixes the first to indicate "no travel" and the second to indicate a way out. The word play, then, is something like, "We have no way to go, but we do have a way out." A paraphrase which would capture the spirit of the word play would be, "We have no way to win, but we are not at a loss." Scripture reminds us of this truth by telling us that "God is faithful, who will not suffer you to be tempted above that ye are able; but will with the temptation also make a way to escape, that ye may be able to bear it" (1 Corinthians 10:13, KJV).

Third, Paul writes that we are "persecuted but not forsaken." Again his play on words clearly illustrates a paradox. We are pursued, but never left behind. That is a comforting thought, especially in such a fast-paced world as the one in which we live. We feel chased after, as if we are about to be run down and rolled over. The Lord, though, has promised us His protection, which is His presence. He will never leave us, nor forsake us. You may be abducted by men, but you'll never be abandoned by God.

Last, Paul says that we are "cast down but not destroyed." The word translated "cast down" means "to throw down" and sometimes implies violence. The Revised Version reads "smitten down." The experience of failure does that to us. We feel rejected and beaten. Your child comes home from school downcast. Your husband comes home from work downtrodden. Your wife ends the day feeling unappreciated and let down. However, Paul says, we're "not destroyed," literally, "not perished." While we may get knocked down, we are never knocked out. We may get thrown down, but we are never pinned. We may have to take a standing eight-count, but we'll never be counted out.

It is not that we are never beaten, just that we are never defeated. We will lose some battles, but we have already won the war! If we fall (or fail), we will rise up and try it again. The whole of Paul's teaching in 2 Corinthians 4:8 and 9 can be summarized by saying that the true Christian is like a

Timex watch: "It takes a licking but it keeps on ticking."

James L. Christensen wrote, "The purpose of Christianity is not to avoid difficulty, but to produce a character adequate to meet it when it comes. It does not make life easy, rather, it tries to make us great enough for life."[2]

The world must see this in us. Our neighbors need to witness this type of optimism and resiliency in the very face of chaotic pressures. They must see see us firmly established in an unshakable joy of the Lord. They must see us crowded but never crushed; cornered but never confined; chased but never caught; and cast down but never carried out.

V. Raymond Edman in an article entitled "The Discipline of Durability" wrote, "To be torn unmercifully by external forces, and still to preserve one's poise, and position, and especially one's inward integrity, is to know the discipline that endures."[3]

Paul knew that discipline. Joseph, in an Egyptian cell, knew that discipline. David in the caves of Engedi knew it, and so did Daniel in the palace towers. Men and women throughout the Bible and history in the face of oncoming difficulties took courage in their God. We, like them, must come to learn that sanctified afflictions can be spiritual promotions. These are times, not to quit, but to bounce back.

In the cartoon strip "B.C.," two cavemen are leaning against a big boulder and they are discussing golf. A prehistoric set of golf clubs are set next to the obvious golf pro, and he is explaining to the other fellow, "Two under par is an eagle. One under par is a birdie. One over par is a bogey. Two over par is a double bogey."

The layman interrupts, "What's ten over par?"

The pro responds smugly, "A reason to quit."

Perhaps you think you have ample reason to quit. There will be many who will advise you to do just that. People like Job's wife with a "curse God and die" mentality are plentiful. The pessimists forecasting failure are everywhere. But don't give up or give in. Cheer up, even if the worst is yet to come. Allow them the opportunity to see you model Christlike character while going through tough times. Setbacks are no reason to sit back, and putdowns are no reason to stay down.

Suggestions and Summary

- Study the life of Joseph in Egypt (Genesis 37-50). Attempt to catalog all the examples of optimism expressed by Joseph during the times of trial and imprisonment.
- Memorize the following Scripture texts: Psalm 62:6; Micah 7:8; Romans 8:28; Romans 8:18; Romans 8:35-39 and 2 Corinthians 4:17.
- The optimist is wrong probably as often as the pessimist is, but the optimist has a lot more fun.

TWELVE

PLANNING TO FAIL?

THERE IS AN OLD AXIOM which states that if you fail to plan, you have planned to fail. Another can be added to that: If you aim at nothing, you can't miss.

Perhaps if not all that awe-inspiring, these little statements do, at least, communicate sound advice. It has been the stated premise of this book to look at failure in a way that we might benefit from it. While it makes good sense to learn from failure, it makes no sense to invite it.

Succeeding is nothing more than following through on a plan. Failure, on the other hand, is usually the result of a poorly devised plan, or no plan at all.

Good planning means setting goals. And goal setting, to be effective, must be understood. A goal, simply defined, is an end toward which you are going to direct effort. Goals can be short term, such as getting to bed by 10:00 tonight; or they can be long term, such as graduating from medical school and becoming a doctor.

Goals are essential in that they help us not only to define better what it is we want to accomplish, but they also direct us and keep us on track.

Goal setting can be fun, and it can also be demanding. The Word of God gives us many glimpses of goal setters.

Abraham was a goal setter, and so was Moses. Caleb is one of the clearest examples of setting a goal and sticking to it. He set his sights on Mount Hebron, and declared to Joshua, "I want that mountain." With the objective clearly in front of him, it was not long before Hebron was Caleb's for an inheritance (Joshua 14).

One of the greatest illustrations of the determination it takes to carry through on a goal can be seen in the reference to Christ as setting His face steadfastly to go to Jerusalem (Luke 9:53).

Undoubtedly, Paul understood goals. Beck translates 1 Corinthians 9:26 as Paul saying, "I run with a clear goal before me."[1] Paul rarely allowed anything to disrupt the pursuit of the goals he had established (Acts 20:24). His classic statement to the Philippian church gives us a glimpse of his determination to achieve his goals, "Forgetting those things which are behind, and reaching forth unto those things which are before, I press toward the mark for the prize of the high calling of God in Christ Jesus" (Philippians 3:13,14, KJV).

Goals can be either long term or short term, and we should have some of both. The benefit of a long-range goal is that it gives us the time to develop our strategy. It gives us something to work for, and allows us the opportunity to experiment. Long-range goals give me the broader view, and while I lose a battle or two, I can still see that the war can be won. Charles Noble once said, "You must have long-range goals to keep you from being frustrated by short-range failures."[2] That is sound advice.

A perfect time to generate some long-term goal setting is when your children reach junior high and high school. As teenagers, they will need some questions answered about vocations. In late junior high and early high school years the time is right to help them plan some goals for a life's work. Often in their senior year, all of a sudden teenagers will decide what they think they would like to do, and then find to their dismay that they lack certain essential training. A steady schedule of wood shop will not be much of an advantage to your high school senior who has just decided he wants to become a doctor.

Help your children set some long-range goals while still in their teenage years. Challenge them, prod them, motivate them, help them along. If we fail to do this, we are just assisting our children to wander through life aimlessly.

Short-term goals are necessary also. While long-range goals give you the bigger picture, short-term goals provide the excitement and stimulation of immediate achievements. All long-range goals and no short-term ones might make life a little dull and top heavy.

Obviously, short-term goals can be building blocks to that one great long-term goal that you have chosen. After striking out in a game, Charlie Brown pours out his heart to Lucy, "I'll never be a big-league player! I just don't have it! All my life I've dreamed of playing in the big leagues, but I know I'll never make it!"

Lucy replies, "You're thinking too far ahead, Charlie Brown. What you need to do is to set yourself more immediate goals. Start with the next inning, for example. When you go out to pitch, see if you can walk out to the mound — without falling down."

That's us! We want to make it to the big leagues, but we find we're having trouble just getting out to the mound. Short-term goals are the answer.

The way this works is not all that difficult. For example, if your goal is to read the entire Bible over the next year, you will want to set a few short-term goals (or indicators), so that you can gauge your progress. You could, for instance, divide the Bible into twelve sections, and then each month check your progress by seeing where you are in comparison to those sections. If after five months you are still struggling through the genealogies in the book of Numbers, you'll know you're in trouble. Like the little seven-year-old girl who wrote to her pastor, "I read the bibel every day since I was a Little kid. So far I am up to the first page. Sincrely, Melissa."

Goal setting can be an interesting process, but there are some guidelines that need to be understood. The first rule is that all goals should be realistic. We violate this principle in two ways. Either we set a goal that is so far out of reach that there is no way to attain it, or we state something as a goal that really is not one at all.

The child of God who declares his goal is to get to heaven has not stated a real goal, in that heaven is an assured fact for the redeemed. If you have received Christ, you are going to heaven, whether it is your stated goal or not. A better long-range goal for the Christian is to become Christlike in character. Now you can install a number of short-term goals which will assist you in leading a Christ-like life — Bible-reading, prayer time, service, and so on.

A realistic goal is basically a reachable goal. It is not one that is so bizarre as to be impossible to attain. Part of goal setting is the reward of achieving.

If your goals are consistently unrealistic and therefore unreachable, you will continually be experiencing defeat and frustration.

A second guideline is that all goals should have deadlines. Goals stated without target dates are only tasks. For example, if I say that my goal is to fix my leaky faucet, and simply leave it at that, I have not stated a goal, I have only identified a task to be done. If I say that I will fix my leaky faucet by Friday afternoon at 5 P.M., I have stated it as a goal; for I have specified the dimension of completion. In our churches we declare that our goal is evangelism. Stated that way, evangelism is only a task; it does not become a goal until someone provides the time and place, who is going out and when, and how many people are to be visited and where.

Many of our goals then are not goals at all; they are tasks and dreams. Unless we state our goals in terms of when, where, how and with what, we are not stating goals effectively. More often than not, tasks go unfinished, and dreams never take on substance.

A well-stated goal, on the other hand, has an objective, which is stated as a result, and then I know what it is and when to expect its completion. I have put in various target indicators to check my progress. If need be, I can adjust my target indicators, without ever having to alter my goal.

For Christians, another important guideline is that our goals must be based upon righteousness. This must be a priority in the planning of any goal. The Lord Jesus said, "Seek first his kingdom and his righteousness" (Matthew 6:33). Paul wrote, "Set your minds on things above, not on earthly things" (Colossians 3:2).

Our goal setting must reflect a spirituality that is Holy Spirit motivated. Carnal goals will lack God's blessing. Plans that are based more on the flesh than on the Spirit will produce death rather than life (Romans 8:5,6).

Perhaps it is in this one area, goal setting, that we can reflect the character of Christ more effectively than in any other. The world needs to see us working out in a spiritually dynamic way both our short-term and long-range goals. They need to see that what we want to accomplish is based on what we are supposed to be. Our agenda is not one of dog-eat-dog and step on whoever gets in the way, but it is one motivated by a hungering and thirsting after righteousness. Our goals must reflect His grace.

Goals are necessary. Godly goals are imperative. The church needs goals once again. Without clear and dynamic goals the church is doomed to mediocrity. Without goals the church offers activity, and in turn that activity is made synonymous with spirituality. If we are busy, we "must be spiritual." Nothing could be further from the truth.

Goals will help us define not only who we are, but why we are, what we are supposed to be doing, and when we are to do it. Goals will help us be creative, and because we were made in God's image, creativity is a birthright.

There will be many obstacles to overcome in the pursuit of your goals. There always are. The Word of God says "press on" (Philippians 3:14; 1 Corinthians 15:58; Galatians 6:9). The Lord encourages us to keep our hands on the plow and not look back (Luke 9:62). A little boy in Sunday school, upon hearing about how Lot's wife looked back and turned into a pillar of salt, interrupted his teacher and said, "My mother looked back once while she was driving — and she turned into a telephone pole!"

Set some goals. Be sure they are godly, and will please Him. Plan, both for the long range, and the immediate. Work hard. Gauge your progress with target indicators. Adjust whatever needs to be adjusted without losing sight of your main objective. Keep moving on — and watch out for telephone poles.

Suggestions and Summary

- You must begin by setting some goals, so set them. Determine at least one long-range goal, and perhaps five short-term goals. Ask yourself the following questions for each one:
  Is it realistic?
  Is it reachable?
  Is it stated as a result?
  Is it righteous?
- If you have teenagers, sit down and talk with them about their life's work. What would they like to do? How can you help? What goals, both long-term and short can be established right now to start them on the way?
- Utilize "target indicators" for all your goals. Visualize your goal on a timeline and record your progress. If your goal was to read casually through the Bible in the next year, the chart could look something like the following:

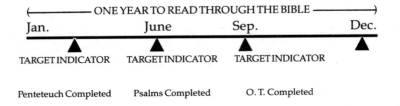

(Note: With Old Testament approximately ¾ of Bible, completion of Old Testament should be targeted for September. With Genesis through the Psalms approximately ⅔ of Old Testament, Psalms should be targeted for completion by end of June; etc.)

- When your goal is to go to "Jerusalem," do not let even well-meaning friends sidetrack you (Acts 21:4,10-12).

THIRTEEN

A COURAGE
TO PERFORM

THE GREAT AUTOMOTIVE GENIUS Henry
Ford once stated that failure is merely an opportunity
to start again.

He is right. But starting over demands courage.
The possibility of failing again is real, and it seems
an even greater risk is involved than before. Yet as
Kenneth Wilson observed, "Fear of failure is the risk
we take for succeeding."

The nation of Israel had to start again. They
had failed miserably. They were supposed to march
right in and possess the land that flowed with milk
and honey. Instead, however, they backed off, and
kept backing up, as it were, for forty years.

Years later, they were ready to start again. Joshua
was in command. All the rebels had died off, and
the nation was ready to succeed where once they
had failed. And what do you suppose the Lord's
primary message to them was?

"Be strong and courageous" (Joshua 1:6).

"Be strong and very courageous" (Joshua 1:7).

"Have not I commanded you? Be strong and courageous. Do not be terrified" (Joshua 1:9).

To succeed where once you failed, the major ingredient must be courage. A courage to perform.

In spite of failure.

In spite of the risks.

In spite of the fears.

Winston Churchill leaves us that type of courageous legacy. At the conclusion of the crucible of World War II, Churchill was asked to give a commencement speech at his boyhood alma mater (a school, incidentally, where he almost flunked out.)

Upon being introduced with all the accolades that might be expected for the bulldog of British resolve, the great statesman approached the podium, looked out over the student body and then delivered his speech. It was only nine words: "Never give up. Never give up — never, never, never." He then returned to his seat as the audience pondered the impact of his words.

Could any speech be more moving? Could anyone have summed up more succinctly than that the steadfastness and courage we so desperately need in our lives? The greatest failure is to stop trying. The biggest sin is to give up.

"Though a righteous man falls seven times, he rises again" (Proverbs 24:16).

"Do not gloat over me, my enemy! Though I have fallen, I will rise" (Micah 7:8).

Captain Eddie Rickenbacker was once asked why it seemed that nothing could defeat him. He replied, "My mother taught her kids to pray, to read the Bible, to follow Jesus Christ, and never to give up."[1]

Similarly, C.C. Cameron challenges us:

A little more persistence, courage,
  vim,
Success will down o'er failure's
  cloudy rim.
Then take this honey for the bit-
  terest cup;
There is no failure, save in giving
  up.
No real fall, so long as one still
  tries,
For seeming set-backs make the
  strong man wise.
There's no defeat, in truth, save
  from within;
Unless you're beaten there, you're
  bound to win.[2]

We must understand what courage really is. Courage, first of all, is not the absence of fear. Somehow we have the idea that courage is some mindless insensitivity to the reality of danger. We believe it to be a blind, macho-type attitude whose credo is always, "Damn the torpedoes — full speed ahead."

The courageous, we believe, must have ice water in their veins, or hearts made of steel and wills forged out of iron.

Actually, real courage is simply getting a job done in spite of fear. Courage is like faith, and therefore must be active. Courage grows by action. It becomes pronounced because of performance.

Therefore, courage is not the absence of fear: rather, it is the presence of faith. It is a belief in what you are doing, like Nehemiah's (Nehemiah 6:3). It is a belief that God is with you as you do it, like Joshua's (Joshua 1:9). It is, ultimately, the belief that God is able to get it done, like Paul's (Philippians 1:6).

Yes, it takes courage to keep on.

It takes courage not to want to quit.

It takes faith to try — and try — and try again if need be.

Unfortunately, it seems that too many Christians are content not only not to try again, but not to try at all. Nevertheless, the message of God's Word continues to be like a half-time locker-room pep talk, pushing us on, cheering us on, challenging us to get back out there and win one for the Lord!

Can we afford not to go?

Can we survive by not trying?

Consider the alternatives.

The Bible warns us of the dangers of carnal fear and cowardice. Fear, like cancer, siphons away our strength and spiritual vitality.

These are the two extremes: a life of faith, or a life of fear. A courage to perform, or a contentment to stay safe. A rising to serve the Lord, or a sliding back down into obscurity.

The two extremes can be seen in 1 Samuel 17, where young David came to bring his soldier brothers some supplies, only to find them, along with the rest of the army, cowering in their foxholes under the verbal bombardment of Goliath. With the Philistine army cheering their gigantic champion on, the gauntlet was thrown down for anyone in Israel to pick up. None dared.

That is, until David, in righteous rebuke of Israel's willingness to let God's name be blasphemed, marched out to face Goliath with just a staff, a sling and five smooth stones. And where was David's confidence? In the armor of man? Never! He refused Saul's. His courage was motivated by an abiding faith in the God who had delivered him in times past from lion and bear. "This uncircumcised Philistine," David declared, "will be like one of them" (1 Samuel 17:36).

I have often wondered what the rest of the troops must have felt like after God gave the victory single-handedly to David, while they stayed safely tucked away in their foxholes. They had allowed themselves to be frozen by fear, rendered inactive by danger. If not for a shepherd boy's courage, it would have been a miserable day of futility.

The soldiers had made their choice, and now you can make yours — life on the firing line or in the safety of the foxhole. Safety demands we forfeit glory. Mediocrity demands we forfeit creativity. A life of apathy means missing out on the appropriation of God's choicest blessings. Are we willing to pay that price? An old poem has it:

> Had Moses failed to go, had God
> Granted his prayer, there would
>   have been
> For him no leadership to win;
> No pillared fire; no magic rod;
> No wonders in the land of Zin;
> No smiting of the sea; no tears
> Ecstatic shed on Sinai steep;
> No Nebo, with a God to keep
> His burial; just forty years
> Of desert, watching with his
>   sheep.[3]

If we could only catch that spirit today. With a spirit of courage and resolve and a never-say-die attitude toward serving the Lord, there's no telling what could be accomplished!

Where are the Davids pastoring our churches today? Where are the Nehemiahs, the Aquilas and Priscillas among our lay leaders today? In the face of danger, do you respond with faith or with fear? The message of God's Word is clear enough. We are to walk by faith, not by sight. As a people of God, we are to compare, not ourselves to the giants, but the giants to God!

Reckless you say? Absolutely!

"The people who know their God shall be stead-
fast and will accomplish notable feats" (Daniel 11:32,
Berkley version).

C. T. Studd once lamented, "Are gamblers for
gold so many and gamblers for God so few?" This
is the same great missionary who, when cautioned
about returning to Africa for fear of death, responded
by shouting, "Praise God, I have been looking for
a chance to die for Jesus!" This is the same "fanatic"
who would write:

> Some wish to live within the
>   sound
>   of church or chapel bell,
> I want to run a rescue shop
>   within a yard of hell."[4]

Where are the C. T. Studds today who have a
courage to perform, and are not intimidated by fear
or failure? Where are the Epaphrodituses who are
willing to risk their very lives at the "throw of the
dice" (Philippians 2:30)?

Where are men like Barnabas who are ready to
hazard their lives for the name of our Lord Jesus
Christ (Acts 15:26)? Where are the Pauls, who, in
the face of all opposition and obvious destruction,
stand at the bow of the ship and boldly declare, "I
believe God!" (Acts 27:25)? Where are they who have
learned:

> In the darkest night of the year
> When the stars have all gone out
> That COURAGE is better than
>   fear
> That FAITH is truer than doubt.
>   (Author unknown)

Listen to Teddy Roosevelt, who delivered the following remarks in a speech in Chicago on April 10, 1899:

It is not the critic who counts: not the man who points our how the strongman stumbled or where the doer of deeds could have done them better. The credit belongs to the man who is actually in the arena; whose face if marred by dust and sweat and blood; who strives valiantly; who errs, and comes short again and again, because there is no effort without error and shortcoming; who does actually try to do the deed; who knows the great enthusiasm, the great devotion and spends himself in a worthy cause; who, at the worst, if he fails, at least fails while daring greatly.

Far better it is to dare mighty things, to win glorious triumphs even though checkered by failure, than to rank with those poor spirits who neither enjoy nor suffer much because they live in the gray twilight that knows neither victory nor defeat.

A mistake usually proves that someone has stoped talking long enough to do something. Take the risk to make mistakes. Have the courage to start again. Better it is to get up when knocked down!

To stand up than stay down!
To keep on than give up!
To hold on than drop out!
To move on than roll over!
No one is beaten till he quits,
No one is through till he stops.
No matter how hard failure hits,
No matter how often he drops,
A fellow is not down till he lies
In the dust and refuses to rise.

Fate may bang him around
And batter him till he is sore,
But it is never said that he's down
While he bobs up for more.
A fellow is not dead till he dies,
Nor done till he no longer tries.
                    (Author unknown)

Suggestions and Summary

- The key to triumph is still in the first syllable.
- Courage is not the absence of fear, it is the presence of faith — a faith to perform in the very face of fear (John 1:5-9); Deuteronomy 31:6; Hebrews 13:5; Acts 27:1-25).
- Seek to gain a knowledge of God's promises, which will lead you to acknowledge His presence. Appreciate that God's presence dwarfs all the "giants" of circumstances against you (Hoses 4:6; Romans 10:17; 2 Corinthians 5:7; Romans 8:31; 1 Peter 3:13).
- Remember that the one who says "I can't," and the one who says "I can," are *both* right!
- "God is not looking for nibblers of the possible, but for grabbers of the impossible."[5]
- "Success isn't final, failure isn't fatal; it's courage that counts."[6]

POSTSCRIPT
The Race[1]

"Quit!" "Give up, you're beaten,"
They shout and plead;
"There's just too much against you now,
This time you can't succeed."

And as I start to hang my head
In front of failure's face,
My downward fall is broken
By the memory of a race.

And hope refills my weakened will
As I recall that scene.
For just the thought of that short race
Rejuvenates my being.

A children's race, young boys, young men;
Now I remember well
Excitement, sure, but also fear;
It wasn't hard to tell.

They all lined up so full of hope
Each thought to win that race
Or tie for first, or if not that,
At least take second place.

And fathers watched from off the side,
Each cheering for his son.
And each boy hoped to show his dad
That he would be the one.

The whistle blew and off they went,
Young hearts and hopes on fire.
To win, to be the hero there,
Was each young boy's desire.

And one boy in particular,
His dad was in the crowd,
Was running near the lead and thought,
"My dad will be so proud."

But as he speeded down the field,
Across a shallow dip,
The little boy who thought to win,
Lost his step and slipped.

Trying hard to catch himself,
His hands flew out to brace,
And mid the laughter of the crowd,
He fell flat upon his face.

So, down he fell and with him hope,
He couldn't win it now.
Embarrassed, sad, he only wished
To disappear somehow.

But, as he fell, his dad stood up
And showed his anxious face
Which to the boy so clearly said,
"Get up and win that race!"

He quickly rose, no damage done,
Behind a bit, that's all,
And ran with all his mind and might
To make up for his fall.

So, anxious to restore himself,
To catch up and to win,
His mind went faster than his legs.
He slipped and fell again.

He wished that he had quit before
With only one disgrace.

"I'm hopeless as a runner now,
I shouldn't try to race."

But, in the laughing crowd he searched
And found his father's face.
That steady look that said again,
"Get up and win that race."

So, he jumped up to try again,
Ten yards behind the last,
"If I'm going to gain those yards," he thought,
"I've got to run real fast."

Exceeding everything he had,
He regained eight or ten,
But trying so hard to catch the lead,
He slipped and fell again.

Defeat! He lay there silently,
A tear dropped from his eye.
"There's no sense running anymore.
Three strikes, I'm out — why try."

The will to rise had disappeared,
All hope had fled away.
So far behind, so error prone,
Closer all the way.

"I've lost so what's the use," he thought,
"I'll live with my disgrace."
But then he thought about his dad;
Who soon he'd have to face.

"Get up," an echo sounded low.
"Get up and take your place.
You're not meant for failure here,
Get up and win that race."

With borrowed will, "Get up," it said,
    "You haven't lost at all,
For winning's not more than this —
    To rise each time you fall."

So up he rose to win once more.
    And with a new commit,
He resolved that win or lose,
    At least he wouldn't quit.

So far behind the others now,
    The most he'd ever been.
Still he gave it all he had
    And ran as though to win.

Three times he'd fallen, stumbling,
    Three times he rose again.
Too far behind to hope to win,
    He still ran to the end.

They cheered the winning runner
    As he crossed, first place,
Head high and proud and happy;
    No falling, no disgrace.

But, when the fallen youngster,
    Crossed the line, last place,
The crowd gave him the greater cheer
    For finishing the race.

And even though he came in last,
    With head bowed low, unproud,
You would have thought he won the race,
    To listen to the crowd.

And to his dad he sadly said,
    "I didn't do so well."

"To me you won," his father said,
"You rose each time you fell."

And now when things seem dark and hard
And difficult to face,
The memory of that little boy
Helps me in my race.

For all of life is like that race,
With ups and downs and all,
And all you have to do to win
Is rise each time you fall.

"Quit!" "Give up, you're beaten,"
They still shout in my face.
But, another voice within me says,
"Get up and finish the race."

- Author unknown

NOTES

Preface
1. Michael Korda, *Success: How Every Man and Woman Can Achieve It* (New York: Random House, 1977), p.4.
2. A. W. Tozer, *Born After Midnight* (Harrisburg, PA: Christian Publications, 1959), p.57.

Chapter 1
1. Anthony Campolo, Jr., *The Success Fantasy* (Wheaton, IL: Victor, 1980), p.9.
2. A. W. Tozer, *Born After Midnight* (Harrisburg, PA: Christian Publications, 1959), p.56.
3. Jess Moody, *A Drink at Joel's Place* (Waco, Tx: Word, 1967), p.86.

Chapter 2
1. Michel Quoist, *The Meaning of Success* (South Bend, IN: Fides, 1963), p.79.
2. Thomas Tutko and William Bruns, *Winning Is Everything and Other American Myths* (New York: Macmillan, 1976), p. 197.
3. Ibid., pp.4-5.

Chapter 3
1. Stan Mooneyham, "Bearing One Another's Burdens," *World Vision* (December 1981), p.23.
2. Henry J. Foster, *The Preacher's Homiletic Commentary* (on the Epistles of St. Paul the Apostle to the Corinthians) (New York: Funk & Wagnalls, n.d.), p.499.
3. A. B. Bruce, *The Training of the Twelve* (New York: Doubleday, 1928), p.13.

4. Henry Wadsworth Longfellow, quoted by Virginia Ely in *I Quote* (title unknown) (New York: George W. Stewart Publisher, Inc., 1947), p.377.
5. Findley B. Edge, from my notes, quoted by a college professor during a lecture in a Christian education course.

Chapter 4
1. Debbie Ritchie, "Lessons From Lincoln," *Pulpit Helps* (February 1981) 6:5:10.

Chapter 6
1. C. William Fisher, *It's Revival We Need* (Kansas City, MO: Nazarene Publishing House, 1966), p.35.
2. D. G. Kehl, "Burnout: The Risk of Reaching Too High," *Christianity Today* (November 20, 1981), p.26.
3. Ibid.
4. John W. Gardiner, "The Things You Learn After You Know It All," *Reader's Digest* (September 1980), p.147.
5. Michel Quoist, *The Meaning of Success* (South Bend, IN: Fides, 1963), p.16.
6. J. Allen Blair, *Living Patiently* (Neptune, NJ: Loizeaux, 1966), pp.108-9.
7. Richard Weiss, *The American Myth of Success* (New York: Basic Books, 1969), p.172.
8. Phillips Brooks, quoted in *The Encyclopedia of Religious Quotations*, ed. Frank S. Mead (Old Tappan, NJ: Fleming H. Revell Co., 1976), p.354.

Chapter 7
1. Bernard Ruffin, *Fanny Crosby* (NY: United Church Press, a Pilgrim Progress book, 1976), p.236.

2. M. Mannington Dexter, "Joseph," *Springs in the Valley* by Mrs. Charles E. Cowman (Minneapolis: World Wide Publications, 1980), p.228.
3. Michel Quoist, *The Meaning of Success* (South Bend, IN: Fides, 1963), p.77.
4. Violet Alleyn Storey, "Tea in an Old House," *The Greatest Men of the Bible* by Clarence E. Macartney (New York: Abingdon-Cokesbury Press, 1941), p.19.
5. Zig Ziglar, *See You at the Top* (Gretna: Pelican Publishing Co., 1977), p.149.

Chapter 8
1. Quoted by Mrs. Charles E. Cowman, *Streams in the Desert* (Minneapolis: World Wide Publications, 1979), p.274.
2. Andrae Crouch, "Through It All." © Copyright 1971 by Manna Music, Inc., 2111 Kenmere Ave., Burbank, CA 91504. International copyright secured. All rights reserved. Used by permission.

Chapter 9
1. I am unable to document the source of this quote. I believe it was in a newspaper article.
2. William Marston, "Take Your Profits From Defeat," *Pulpit Helps* (April 1984) 10:7:12.
3. Dave Breese, *Life's Not What I Thought* (Lincoln, NE: Back to the Bible, 1978), p.49.
4. Ella Wheeler Wilcox, "Resolve," *The Supplementary Bible* (Chicago: Buxton-Westerman, 1928), p.543.
5. Quoted by Fredelle Maynard, "Turning Failure Into Success," *Reader's Digest* (December 1977), p.126.

Chapter 10
1. Vernon C. Grounds, "Faith for Failure," *Seminary Study Series* (Denver: Conservative Baptist Theological Seminary, 1977), p.3.
2. Ibid., p.5.
3. A. W. Tozer, *Born After Midnight* (Harrisburg, PA: Christian Publications, 1959), p.59.
4. Paul E. Adolph, *Release From Tension* (Chicago: Moody, 1956), p.76.
5. Frank S. Mead, ed., *The Encyclopedia of Religious Quotations* (Old Tappan, NJ: Revell, 1976), p.681.
6. Ibid., p. 58.
7. Meeler Markham, *The Confident Faith* (Nashville: Broadman, 1968), p.106.
8. Clovis G. Chappell, *Faces About the Cross* (New York: Abingdon, 1941), p.31.
9. Tozer, *Born After Midnight*, p.48.
10. Woodrow Wilson, quoted in *Encyclopedia of 7700 Illustrations* by Paul Lee Tan (Rockville, MD: Assurance Publishers, 1979), p.1375.

Chapter 11
1. A. W. Tozer, *The Root of the Righteous* (Harrisburg, PA: Christian Publications, 1955), p.156.
2. Frank S. Mead, ed., *The Encyclopedia of Religious Quotations* (Old Tappan, NJ: Fleming H. Revell Co., 1976), p.97.
3. V. Raymond Edman, *The Disciplines of Life* (Minneapolis: World Wide Publications, 1948), p.237.

Chapter 12
1. *The New English Bible* (New York: Cambridge University Press, 1961).
2. Eleanor L. Doan, ed., *The Speaker's Sourcebook* (Grand Rapids: Zondervan, 1960), p.1120.

Chapter 13

1. Norman Vincent Peale, *Try Never Giving Up* (Pawling, NY: Foundation for Christian Living, 1978), p.27.
2. William Barrett Millard, ed., *The Supplementary Bible*, 544.
3. J. R. Miller, quoted in *Springs in the Valley* by Mrs. Charles E. Cowman (Minneapolis: World Wide Publications, 1980), p.63.
4. Norman Grubb, *C. T. Studd, Cricketer and Pioneer* (Chicago: Moody Press, 1962), p.160.
5. Ibid., p.159.
6. Winston Churchill quoted in *Pulpit Helps* (April 1984), 10:7:12.

Postscript

1. "The Race" is a poem I heard quoted over KMPC/AM Radio by Scott St. James in 1981. I wrote and requested a copy, which was sent to me with the author listed as unknown.